LETTERS *for* HEALING

REVISED EDITION

LETTERS *for* HEALING

The Therapeutic Power
of Writing to a Lost Loved One

VON KOPFMAN C.M.P.

Letters for Healing
By Von Kopfman

Edited by Gary Marx
Book design by D.J. Hyde Matheny

Published by MISSION POINT PRESS
2554 Chandler Road
Traverse City, MI 49696
All rights reserved.
Copyright © 2022 Von Kopfman

Second edition, first printing

ISBN: 978-1-958363-12-6 (hardcover)
ISBN: 978-1-958363-13-3 (softcover)

Library of Congress number 2013933682
Printed in the United States.

Copies of this book are available online at Amazon.com and other online sellers, and wherever ine books are sold.

If you or someone you know has lost a child, grandchild, or sibling, please visit www.forthesurvivors.org

The author is accepting submission for future editions. Please email your letter and contact info to forthesurvivors@hotmail.com

 The Letters Project Book   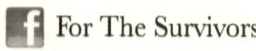 For The Survivors

LETTERS *for* HEALING

"A letter always seemed to me like immortality."

– EMILY DICKINSON

PREFACE

At 7:40 A.M. ON August 11, 2011, my son, Jacob Von Kopfman, bought two slices of breakfast pizza, two bottles of Gatorade and a can of Skoal. By 9:30 a.m., he was gone. This was the beginning of my worst nightmare, and my worst fear come true. In our small community of 3,000, Jacob had lost one friend in December of 2007 and four more friends in the 20 months prior to his own death. In fact, two of those friends had died just a couple of weeks before. I had attended funerals and seen the hurt and the blank expressions. I sympathized with the parents' loss, but I was always grateful it was not one of my children. As a parent, you think you can imagine what the pain of losing a child must feel like. You cannot.

The moment that Jacob died, I could not think. I didn't know what to do, whom to call or where to turn. I was vulnerable, scared and scarred in ways that I had never imagined possible.

I received a lot of useless and often frustrating advice from people who meant well, but really just had no idea what to say. I needed help, and I realized that I wasn't alone in struggling to navigate through the loss of a child. I decided that in order to survive the loss of Jacob, I had to find a way to make something positive out of the pain and confusion. I needed to find a way to help people trying to survive the tragedy of losing a loved one.

I met with 40 families who had lost a child, and I got their input. I found information, resources and tools that could guide a person dealing with the loss of a child. Finally, I interviewed and gathered information from three well-respected psychologists. Through this exploration, www.forthesurvivors.org was born. The goal was to work with schools, hospitals, military branches, police and fire departments, funeral homes and hospice centers to make this information available to as many parents as possible at the moment they needed it the most.

At the same time, I realized I was in need of healing. My surviving son and Jacob's identical twin brother, Jordan, and I began meeting separately with Dr. Jon Farrell-Higgins after Jacob's death. Jordan was angry that he wasn't able to tell his brother goodbye. Dr. Farrell-Higgins suggested that Jordan write a letter to Jacob telling him everything that was left unsaid.

Jordan found writing the letter beneficial; so I wrote a letter, too. It was so helpful that I then suggested to my daughter Kierston, my parents, and the parents in our community who had recently lost children that they write letters as well. Everyone found some comfort and healing through the process.

As a songwriter, I found the words of the letters to be so powerful that upon the suggestion of Jordan, I turned the letters written by my family members into songs. I then offered to do the same for the other families. The letters and the music have helped my healing process by helping others on their own journey toward healing.

Grief is not a straight line, and while it certainly has a clear beginning it has no predictable end. Everyone handles grief differently, yet there appear to be five definable stages: denial/isolation, anger, bargaining, depression, and finally acceptance. I have found myself experiencing the first four at various times, I'm not sure I have fully accepted it yet.

Before I lost Jacob, I had known only a handful of people who had lost a child. Now I know many, too many. I realized that it would be selfish to limit what had become known as "The Letters Project" to just our small group. I realized that the need is great and the resources are few, which led to the book you are holding now.

It is my hope that through the www.forthesurvivors.org website and this book that you will feel a little less alone, find the resources you need, and lighten your load. I dedicate this book to all those lost and to all of you, the survivors.

VON KOPFMAN

In Memory of:

ANDREW FUTRELL: 4/17/1990 - 12/4/2007

KIRK MANWARING: 3/26/1984 - 1/9/2010

COLE AUGUSTYN: 2/14/1992 - 3/12/2011

SKYLER HIVELY: 4/15/1990 - 7/24/2011

BEN BURKE: 2/20/1992 - 7/28/2011

JACOB KOPFMAN: 5/8/1990 - 8/11/2011

FOREWORD

THROUGH WRITING LETTERS TO LOVED ONES who have passed, I have been able to express anger, grief, loss, and joy without any judgment. I've laughed, cried and resolved issues I wasn't able to address in time. I've found the peace in my heart necessary to forgive myself, and recover from my sense of abandonment without guilt. The letters remind me of the lessons I was taught by those I cherish, which has helped to keep them alive in my heart. The writing process itself has helped me clarify who I want to be and the patterns I hope to avoid. By committing my truest emotions to paper, I've learned to be fearless as I've sought personal peace.

Von Kopfman's book may have been borne of the grief from the loss of his son, but it has become a symbol of healing and the start of a community. Our letters are personal and allow us the freedom to express our emotions honestly. Then, by sharing these private feelings, we find that in the depths of our loss we are not alone… we are not isolated — and that itself can help us find a way back. *Letters for Healing* reminds us that no matter how we might be struggling, there are others who have faced similar circumstances and found solace. Von and I have both found the healing power of putting pen to paper. I hope this book encourages you to do the same.

Namaste.

GREG LOUGANIS
FIVE-TIME OLYMPIC MEDALIST, FIVE-TIME WORLD DIVING CHAMPION

November 12, 2012

INTRODUCTION

"**M**ORE THAN KISSES, LETTERS MINGLE SOULS."

When English poet John Donne penned those words, there was only one way to write a letter: by hand. And despite the technological advances we've made since then, there is still no better way to express our emotions than with a pen and a piece of paper.

The art of hand-writing a letter has been around for centuries. And even today — in a world of texts and tweets, instant messages and emails — nothing stirs the heart like receiving a handwritten letter from a friend or loved one.

As Emily Dickinson said: "A letter is a joy of Earth!"

Evidence has proved that the act of writing a letter by hand is a much more intense experience than any other form of communication. I know this firsthand. There is a mental release of words that is connected to the physical act of writing, which allows the writer to express deep personal thoughts and emotions about the person they are writing to. Typed letters or emails are often more mechanical. Auto-correct has no heart. The imagination is limited by keystrokes and scrollbars.

Samuel Johnson, the brilliant English author and poet, wrote: "In a man's letters you know, Madam, his soul lies naked, his letters are only a mirror of his breast, whatever passes within him is shown undisguised in its natural process. Nothing is inverted, nothing distorted, you see systems in their elements, you discover actions in their motives."

It is very easy when hand-writing a letter to become transported and reveal what is truly in your heart. It is almost as if you are writing in third person what you are experiencing in first person. Hand-writing a letter allows the writer's words to flow freely as an expression of truth.

Handwritten letters preserve the memories of the past and all the emotions that are connected to those memories. Each year an elderly couple that I know selects one love letter, saved from their younger days, to read to the other. The words transport them to those places and feelings they had when the letter was written, and rejuvenates their love for each other.

In *A Woman of Independent Means*, Elizabeth Forsythe Hailey wrote, "Please write again soon. Though my life is filled with activity, letters encourage momentary escape into others' lives, and I come back to my own with greater contentment."

In today's world we do not keep a box of emails or tweets, yet we naturally keep letters written by loved ones. Handwritten letters are like timeless flecks of your heart being spread around to the people you love. They are an expression of feelings that are personal in a way that you would never share on a social networking site or in any email.

THE HEALING POWER OF THE PEN

The act of writing a letter to a person who has passed away is part of a process called narrative therapy.

Writing gives you a chance to share emotions with the loved one who has passed — love, anger, forgiveness, guilt, sorrow, pride, peace, loss. It gives you a chance to say what had not been said, a chance to share a favorite story or memory, a chance to release what is burrowing inside the heart.

People will sometimes bury their feelings about a loss. That seems like a natural thing to do, but nearly always it has an adverse effect. Writing a letter helps. It works. Writing presents an opportunity for survival; it allows you to ponder the mystery of life and death, and the tragedy that can befall any of us.

Many people have told me that while writing a letter they feel closer to the person they are addressing. Relationships do not end just because a loved one has passed, and writing to that person can help maintain a feeling of closeness.

Some parents of deceased children have written ongoing series of letters — sometimes on or near the birth date or date of death. They communicate all that has happened since their passing and how the parent's grief and life has changed as a result. These letters are often reread and shared as part of the healing process.

If you feel comfortable, you may want to share your letter or letters with family members, or with those who have experienced a similar loss. This book is full of such letters.

As I researched this book and worked with survivors, I learned one very important thing: That while all of us who have lost loved ones share a common experience, we all deal with loss differently.

It is important to remember that just because a death may have happened many years ago, no one should assume the survivor has had enough time to "get over it." Time doesn't always heal every wound. It is also important to remember that the loss of a child, grandchild, or sibling is just as devastating regardless of the age or circumstance. Death holds no regard for age, social status, wealth, education, or religion.

I recently had the opportunity to visit with an 85-year-old mother who had lost her 65-year-old son. She told me, "John may have been 65 years old and retired, but he was still my baby."

When you lose a loved one like this, a shadow passes over you. You are overcome with feelings that you cannot possibly go on, writing your letter allows you to pour out all of your emotions, to bare your soul in a way that publicly you may not be ready to.

While the letters in this book are graciously shared, sometimes letters are kept private. That's OK, and those letters still carry the power of healing.

Abraham Lincoln was known for his letter writing and fully understood the power of the pen. He wrote lengthy letters to those he felt had wronged him or misunderstood him, to political foes and enemies of the state. He would write letters to express his anger, argue his position, or even tell the offender off. These letters were then sealed in an envelope and marked "Do Not Send." They were found in his desk drawers and files after his death. The healing power was not so much in having anyone read the letter, the healing power was in the writing.

Lincoln, who lost two sons within his life, wrote to Willie after the boy died of typhoid fever: "My poor boy, you were too good for this earth, God has called you home, I know you are much better off in

Heaven, but we loved you so. It is so hard to have you die!"

Greg Louganis, the Olympic and World champion diver, was asked recently in *Men's Journal*, "How should a man handle loss?" Louganis responded, "I write letters. Losing my mom, losing my dad, losing various dogs … a lot of times there's anger around those losses, so I write it out for myself in a letter to them. All good things that I would want to say and share. And after I write it and I'm able to be at peace, I put the letter in the fire and burn it."

Gregg Allman of the Allman Brothers Band wrote in his biography *My Cross to Bear*, how he dealt with the loss of former manager Phil Walden. "I decided to sit myself down and write a letter to Phil — not about him, but to him, directly. I wrote from the heart, and just laid it all out there on the paper." He goes on to say: "Writing that letter freed my soul, man. I told Phil what needed to be said. I made my peace with him, and it allowed me to close it all out."

What Allman, Louganis and Lincoln have found is that the very act of writing is an act of healing.

Social psychologist James Pennebaker found that by having survivors write about traumatic experiences, they most often reveal a considerable range and depth of emotion in their writing, and though they might report being upset by the experience of writing, they also found it valuable and meaningful.

Gaining some sense of closure, expressing deep emotions, relieving pain, releasing stress and frustration, saying what was left unsaid, staying connected to your loved one — all of that — are benefits of narrative therapy, of letter writing.

How reading can comfort

Not only is it emotionally helpful to write a letter, it is often beneficial to read the letters of others.

Fear, isolation, loneliness, and depression are common when we lose a loved one. But knowing that there are others who have experienced similar losses can be very healing. This is one component of a process called exposure therapy.

When you read about other people's traumatic losses several things can happen:

~ You experience your thoughts and feelings in the safety of a shared community, similar to a group therapy experience.
~ You become more comfortable with your thoughts and feelings related to the loss, realizing what you are thinking and feeling is "normal." You learn to accept your feelings, knowing they aren't unusual for the situation.
~ You learn to differentiate the normal, healthy thoughts, feelings and reactions from the unhealthy ones.
~ You can begin to transform your feelings of helplessness, isolation and misunderstanding into patterns of healing.
~ You can discover how others feel and react, as well as how they cope.

Letters for Healing is a collection of 49 letters that represent the variety of ways we react to the loss of a loved one. While this book is not intended to replace the services of a professional therapist, it does offer a simple method for healing. It exposes the reader to the emotions and thoughts of others who have faced similar incidents in their lives.

Letters for Healing is intended to create an interaction between the writer and reader. And it might inspire you to write a letter of your own.

In reading these letters you may find community, understanding and compassion. As you read these letters, you will find that grief knows no social, ethnic or religious boundaries. Life truly is sometimes unfair. Loss is something we will all experience, and death is the great equalizer.

You are not alone in your grief; we are all on the path toward healing.

VON KOPFMAN

THE LETTERS

I

A Community's Loss

Within a span of 3 ½ years, one small community lost six young men, the heart of a generation.

COLE AVERY AUGUSTYN

February 14, 1992 ~ March 12, 2011

He was the son of Tom Augustyn and Debra Augustyn, and the brother of William.

He graduated from Holton High School, Holton, Kansas. He loved anything where the wind was in his face. He loved farming and he worked on custom harvest crews all over the United States. He worked cattle, loved riding his horse, Skippy, mechanic work and welding. He did not know a stranger.

Cole died in an ATV accident.

Dear Cole,

I miss you so much. Your voice, your laughter and your tears I can never see or hear them again. You are with me every day I breathe in and out, traveling down the trail or road of life. I can't help thinking of you every time I hear Jason Aldean sing songs like "Tattoos on This Town" and "Dirt Road Anthem" as it sounds as if he is singing about you. Do you remember the CD you made in high school? We added Chris Ledoux's song "The Ride" at the end of your CD. We all tear up when that song is played. I had a song I am trying to write that reminds me of you, it is called "Forever Nineteen in the Big Red Taxi," but I cannot finish it. But I wrote this poem right after you was gone and it is called, "Full Throttle Never Half."

> *Where do I begin?*
> *The wind in my face*
> *There I go to the next place*
> *To work or play I must go fast*
> *I never want to be last*
> *Disappointment I may bring upon you*
> *But hey I am not Chris Ledoux*
> *I must go fast now to finish*
> *Full throttle, never half*
> *I can only laugh at those in my dust*
> *I can see clearly*
> *Because the wind is in my face*

You were never a disappointment just heartache at times, but you were a second son of a second son that was loved by everyone — the shop boys, the cowgirls and your families. Miss you every day.

Love,

Dad

FROM: TOM AUGUSTYN, FATHER

BENJAMIN MICHAEL BURKE

February 20, 1992 ~ July 28, 2011

He was the son of William (Mike) Burke and Lorena Burke, and the brother of Tara, Tiffany, and Myca.

He graduated from Burlington High School, Burlington, Kansas. He loved all sports, but his passion was baseball. He pitched left handed, and also played left and center field. Known for his big heart and even bigger smile he truly cared about people and had many friends. He also had a strong faith in God.

Ben drowned while fishing and swimming with friends.

Dear Ben,

I guess I want to start out my letter by saying I'm sorry. I'm sorry for the things I didn't do right.

When I was uneasy and didn't want you to go to the River Dam fishing that day, I should have followed my intuition. When you said I could come down to the river and check on you, I should have, instead of telling myself that I need to trust God to take care of you. I should have realized that maybe God was trying to tell me something.

I've been very angry with myself, even with the murky water that held you trapped, if that makes sense. I've also felt anger at the ambulance workers who took you away before I got to see or touch you, even though I was right there waiting. I had to go find you at the funeral home, after looking at the hospital for you. I felt like that was an awful thing for them to do to me, son.

I begged God to take my breath instead and give you back yours, but he didn't do it. I guess He had his reasons or maybe my faith wasn't strong enough. I would have gladly died for you, son. I just didn't know how to make it happen and keep you safe. I was too late. You know those roller coaster rides that I went on with you, even though I was afraid and dreaded them? My love for you was always stronger than my fear. If I couldn't have saved you in the water, you wouldn't have drowned alone. My love for you would have been stronger than my fear. This your mother knows.

I want you to know you were always such a joy to me, son. I know you had me wrapped around your finger, but I also know how much you loved me. When you would hug and kiss me in front of your baseball team or wherever you were, it would make me feel so proud and happy. I will cherish that feeling, and you, forever.

I miss your hugs and kisses, and words of love. I miss your laughter and the light in your beautiful blue eyes. I miss your teasing and your humor. I miss watching your baseball games and watching movies with you. I long to hear your voice and say, "Watch this, Mama." Now your voice and laughter are gone, and silence fills the air. The feeling of heartbreak prevails.

I always told you that I would be OK in life as long as you and your sisters were OK. But now you're gone, I can't reach you, and I'm not OK, even though I have to be strong for your sister.

Even so, I'm glad that the Lord has you. Of that I have no doubt. Thank you for coming back to visit me in spirit, son, and for your hugs, kisses, and words of love.

I guess I'm selfish and it wasn't enough. It will never be enough. At least I know that in spite of my failures, you still love me. Well, I love you more than life itself and consider you a blessing. I always have and always will.

Till we meet again, lots of love.

Mama

FROM: LORI BURKE, MOTHER

ROBERT "ANDREW" FUTRELL

April 17, 1990 ~ December 4, 2007

He was the son of Brenda and Tim Futrell, and he had two brothers, Adam and his twin, Ryan Allen.

He loved golf and photography, graphic arts and his 1973 Chevy Nova, which he called "The Hoss." He was very social and had many friends. He was out with several of them when he died in a tragic accident.

Andrew was a forgiving soul, and in his spirit the family embraces forgiveness. No one was to blame for his death.

My Dear Son Andrew,

Where do I begin to tell you how I feel? Only two words can really describe my feelings and those two words are "heart" and "broken." Almost five years have gone by without you. Not a day goes by that you don't cross my mind. Never in my life did I ever think I could live without one of my children. I did not think it was survivable. I miss you each and every day of my life and would give anything to have just five more minutes with you.

You were an unexpected blessing from the beginning! We didn't plan to have twins but were blessed with them! As a child you were easy to raise. You weren't ornery and hardly ever got in trouble. I only remember being really mad at you once. That was when you gave Ryan a black eye because you were fighting over who was going to ride in the front seat of the car.

I wonder what you would have done with your life as an adult. I wonder who you would have married and if you would have had children. You were an awesome young man and would have been a great husband and father. I wonder if your children would have had your brown eyes.

Life hasn't been the same without you, but it has gone on. We have been on vacation several times to our favorite canoeing spot at Noel, Missouri. We continue to stay at Shady Beach Campground. That was the last vacation we had with you. I also have fond memories from Beaumont, Kansas. We were on our way to the Bennetts' for

their yearly bonfire. We drove south though Beaumont to check out
the wind turbines. We spent a good hour and a half there taking
pictures and just enjoying our family time together. I have photos
of you and Ryan taking photos of each other. We've also discovered
a new place to visit. Your friends Tyler and Blake took Ryan to
the sand dunes at Waynoka, Oklahoma, just a few months after
losing you. It was good for him to spend time with them. I think
you would have liked going there.

I feel your presence every day. Sometimes it's just a little sign or
memory of you. Sometimes it's when I see that car that you thought
was so cute. Sometimes your phone number pops up here or there. If
I'm lucky I will find a coin to remind me of you. It makes me think
of the poem "Pennies From Heaven." There are constant reminders
of you everywhere.

I am thankful for the time that I spent with you. I am thankful for all
the memories we made together and for all the photos we have of
you. I cherish them with all of my heart! I enjoyed being your mom
for the 17-plus years. I wish I could have had more time with you. I
would give anything to change the situation.

I hope by now you have met up with your dad and grandparents. It's
not easy being here without all of you.

Until we meet again, love & miss you with all of my heart.

Your mom

FROM: BRENDA FUTRELL, MOTHER

SKYLER BROCK HIVELY

April 15, 1990 ~ July 24, 2011

He was the son of Seth and Renee Hively, and the brother of Rawlin.

He graduated from Waverly High School, Waverly, Kansas, and attended Coffeyville Community College on a rodeo scholarship. He was self-employed as a ferrier and a cowboy. From the time he could walk he carried a rope and was an avid horseman. He was a four-year member of the KHSRA, competed in the USTRC world finals twice, the URA, and was named its 2010 rookie of the year. He was loved by all who knew him.

Skyler died in an auto accident.

Dear Skyler,

I'm sitting here in the dark just thinking about you. I sure hope it's warmer in heaven because it's cold here. I love you and miss you. Rawlin would like a hall pass to heaven. Can you make that two?

Today Morgan, Kaylani, Devan, Dad, Jacob, and I rode your horses. It was a beautiful morning for a ride. Blue is a little spoiled so Dad had me ride in small circles, and finally he started to behave. I guess I'm going to have to ride more often so your horses don't get fat and lazy.

Could you tell God to send me that sign? Everywhere I go there is something that reminds me of you, and I have to choke down my tears. I guess I need to cowboy up. I am trying, but it hurts. I just love and miss you lots. I called your phone today just to hear your voice. Why is this happening?

It has been four weeks and the hole in my heart will never heal. Skyler, I love and miss you every second. The next chapter of our lives has been completely erased. I keep telling myself you are off in a roping adventure, and I will soon see you trotting across the pasture on your horse.

My heart is hurting and there is not a second that goes by I don't think about you! I want to hear your voice, I want to hold your hand, but most of all I want one of your big hugs!!!

You lived your dream. You were a true cowboy. You may have ridden off into the sunset, but you'll never ride out of our hearts.

Dad and I can't sleep, it's been an emotional day.

I love you, Skyler Brock, you are always on my mind and forever in my heart!

Mom

FROM: RENEE HIVELY, MOTHER

Skyler,

Hey son, I've been riding your young horses! You did a great job getting that frosty roan mare going! I like her! I love you much and I miss you! I wish I could see you, hug you, talk to you, God, I miss you, Skyler. I think about you all day every day! I will always be proud of the man you became.

The wind is blowing, still there is no rain. Your memory is on my mind and it's driving me insanely filled with pain! I try not to show weakness, but my heart hurts today! I love and miss you.

Snuff came to visit me today, every time he is here I feel like you are near.

Thinking about you Skyler, missing and loving you lots!!

Dad

FROM: SETH HIVELY, FATHER

Skyler,

When we think of you the grass grows tall and the tulips have smiles on their faces like they just beat Mohammad Ali. When you walk to your dog, Snuff, he yells your name and when you see your family and friends you see us cry and every tear counts. Skyler you know that you make horses smile. They will miss you. I feel right now they miss you. When an apple grows on a tree it's because of your smile. You can beat the bright sun with your smile. You are riding in a green pasture with Grandpa and you won the National Finals Rodeo!

Rawlin

FROM: RAWLIN JACKSON HIVELY, 10-YEAR-OLD BROTHER

JACOB VON KOPFMAN

May 8, 1990 ~ August 11, 2011

He was the son of Von Kopfman and Kathy Kopfman and the brother of Kierston and twin brother of Jordan.

Jacob graduated from Burlington High School, Burlington, Kansas, and the Missouri Welding Institute. He worked for Hayden Tower Service. He had many friends, none closer than his brother Jordan, and was known for his generous spirit and his beautiful smile. He loved working on cars, listening to music, playing sports, talking politics, taking road trips and helping people. He never knew a stranger.

Jacob died when he fell from a cell tower he was working on.

Dear Jacob,

It seems my worst fear about you taking this job has come true. Maybe I should have really put my foot down. Maybe I should have said, "No, you're not climbing towers!" I could not do that, you were 20 years old and wanted to work. It broke my heart when you would call after one of your temp welding jobs would end, and you would be so upset. I know you just wanted to work, and to be independent. I shared my concerns but the decision was yours. Jacob, I was so proud of you. I am certain you know I was. I wonder what you were thinking when you fell, if it's true that your whole life passes before your eyes. If it did, I hope it was mostly good. I hope it made you smile in those last moments. You were loved by so many, you touched so many. Jacob, you had a huge heart and such a sweet smile. You loved nothing more than helping someone else. They said you didn't suffer. I guess I take some comfort in that, but damn, I miss you. I hurt. I ache to see you, to talk with you, to hold you. I know that you know how much I loved you. And I know you loved me. We never had any trouble expressing that to each other. Jake, inside a part of me died with you, and I'm dying a little more each day. I keep a smile on my face like some well-worn shirt; I have to be strong for Kierston and Jordan, but I tell you inside I just want to scream, I want to curl up in a ball and just let go. I want to be with you where you are, but I can't, while you are there in eternity I am stuck down here in time. No one on this earth knew me better than you did which makes this separation even harder. You and your brother and sister are everything to me, I feel broken beyond repair with you gone. I hate what this has done to our family. I'm so grateful that you, Jordan, and I had supper on that Sunday night, that you called Granny and Grandpa that day, that you and Jordan worked out together. I'm so grateful for the, "I love you" text on that Tuesday before you passed. I hope you know how grateful I am for the 21 years, 3 months and 3 days I had you; it was an honor. I'll never forget you, my beautiful son. I hope your very last thought was just how much your dad loved you. Because I do!

Dad

P.S. Damn You! Now I have to get a tattoo! LOL

FROM: VON KOPFMAN, FATHER

Hey Bro,

I hit the punching bag to let out the rage, but it never seems to end. I drink to numb the pain, but regardless, still it hurts deep down. I smoke for the stress, yet every day I feel more and more reasons to scream and shout.

I still can remember that day … that call, how unbelievable it was. I thought it was a joke. But, no, it was real. That ride, the calls, texts to people for them to pray … praying is something I hadn't done in a while. How people sent their regards … Jacob, that tough S.O.B, will be fine. But, no, we get there and you're gone. The rage, the depression I felt. Seeing you in that 6 x 6 room, how cold you were. Something that will strain my mind forever, will give me nightmares for years. That moment I sent out those texts, the hundreds of calls, texts, unbelievable … they jammed my phone. Coming home to our friends … then tears flowed along with memories.

I'm tired of crying. Feel like I'm dying 'cause all I wanted was five minutes to tell you, "I love you." You can't leave me, you're the most important thing in the world to me.

You're my twin brother, my best friend. Who will be there to have my back? Who will hit on girls with me? Who will be my best man? Who will be my kids' favorite uncle? Who will be there in my time of need? I feel like half of what I was born to be. I need to find a way to be whole again.

How could you leave me? I ask whoever the higher power is how he could take you away from me. Jacob, I love you. I miss you every day, every second. I hope you never forget how much I love you. Please let me know you are at peace. Shelter me, lead me to where you are and someday I'll join you. Then we'll never be apart.

Always know I love you, Jacob Von Kopfman, FOREVER my twin and my best friend.

Jordan

FROM: JORDAN KOPFMAN, BROTHER

Dear Jacob,

Every day I think about you and I know that you are watching over us. I have always believed in angels. I know that I have never really believed in God for a number of reasons, mostly centered around my childhood and family circumstances. But I have believed that there is someone or something watching over us at all times and I hope and believe that you are one of those angels now. You will always be my guardian angel from this time on.

I remember before you were born, we were so excited to learn that your mom and dad were expecting twins. From the beginning I had trouble telling you and Jordan apart. I was very thankful when we discovered that you had a freckle on your forehead to help us do that. As you got older, I still had trouble telling you apart when you were together, but separately, I could.

Jacob, I always enjoyed our conversations when we would see you or you would come to our house. You would tell me all about your car and your school and your new job. We were so worried about you when you were out on your own. Not just about the tower job, but also with welding and all the times you would get burned.

I know you probably thought we were silly for worrying, but that is a grandparent's prerogative.

Please always keep a watch over all of us and ask God if you can have blue wings so we can always tell you apart from all the other angels.

I love you, Jacob, and I always will. You will always be a part of my heart.

Love, Granny

P.S. Keep a special eye on your dad and on Jordan; they are having such a hard time.

FROM: KAREN KOPFMAN, GRANDMOTHER

Dear Jake,

How do you lose a grandson? You don't, he just temporarily relocates. How does life go on? It goes on to continue the human race. I am confident we will reunite in heaven, but I have no idea of when that will happen. We are hurting because we lost you, but we should be rejoicing because we had you. I am very glad we had you even for just a short time on earth and the memories will go on forever.

Do you know how much we miss you and your really sweet smile? You know you won't be forgotten by anyone who loved you. You were a constant source of pride and your twin brother, Jordan, too. I would tell all of my friends all of the things you do. And I don't forget your sister, so pretty and so sweet. Because you all three are my family and I think that's really neat.

Now you have gone up to heaven, hope you meet your family there. Now they can enjoy you as much as we did down here. Well, you know we will always miss you and wish you were still here. The memories we have of you will last us through the years.

Love,

Grandpa Ray K

From: Ray Kopfman, grandfather

Jacob,

Whenever I see the color blue, I think of you. Somedays it seems as if you have been gone forever and other days it seems you just left us. I try not to think of "what would have been" because I know you would have been a great uncle, father and husband. We all miss you down here, but I hope you are proud of us when you are looking down.

I cannot wait to see you again on the other side.

Love,
Kierston

From: Kierston Kopfman Campos, sister

KIRK WILLIAM MANWARING

March 26, 1984 ~ January 9, 2010

He was the son of Bill Manwaring and his wife, Jackie, and Kim Manwaring; brother of Kyle, Erica, and Heather.

He graduated from Burlington High School, Burlington, Kansas, and attended Allen County Community College on a music scholarship. He worked for Allen Tile Company. He was a passionate musician, playing guitar, bass, sitar, and drums. He enjoyed target shooting, hunting, and fishing, and had many friends.

Kirk died in an auto accident.

Kirk,

Just give me one more anything. Where do I start? And how could
I possibly finish telling you how I feel? I have great memories of
watching you mature into a loving, caring, and sensitive young man.
I want one more memory. It was hard to watch you enter some of
those cloudy years where we drifted, but the love was always there.
Regardless of my disapproval of some of your personal decisions
during those cloudy times, I tried to understand, continued to love,
but always as a father. My conscience is clear as I avoided hard love,
harsh words, and refused to give up parenting. In many ways, you
and I are very much alike, when you were upset I knew why, I knew
what made you happy and how difficult it was for you to accept being
mistreated.

I'm glad you experienced love, traveled to Brazil, maintained relationships with family and enjoyed the simple things that life had to
offer. I appreciate how you always managed to attend family gather-
ings, even if you had to travel hundreds of miles. You had a way of
touching the hearts of many and putting smiles on faces.

I wish that things could have been different during those years where
you needed me the most, but forces beyond our control prevented us
from spending extra time together. I had a lot more to give and offer
you. When I lost my two brothers, I did not support my dad as much
as I should have during those times. I just remember thinking he is
strong, but now I know being strong has nothing to do with it. It will
not lower the pain, sorrow, nor help mend the heart.

I will miss how you said, "hello," how you loved and respected your
brother, the hugs you generously offered to all the family and friends.
I want one more memory. You made your mark by treating others
with respect regardless how they may have treated you, how openly
you offered love to your brother and me, and, of course, your passion
for music and guns.

If I were to search for a regret, it would have to be that I want one more; one more fishing trip together, another hug, shooting guns together, sharing a conversation, listening to you play the guitar, or just watch you display politeness. I will never forget, but would love to hear one more time the way you said "hello" when you entered a room. There were opportunities to share more of these things that pleased me about you, but they did not happen, so that is my regret. I'm proud of your genuine character and disposition. You know how I love you, but I just want one more, one more anything.

Love,

Dad

FROM: BILL MANWARING, FATHER

Dear Kirk,

I wish we had the chance to say goodbye and to let you know how much we loved you. Your death was such a tragedy. The car wreck was bad enough, but what you were put through for the organ donation was unforgivable. I know you would be happy to know that two men with children received your kidneys and are doing well. You had such a big heart. I will always remember your smile with those dimples and your beautiful, blue eyes.

Kirk, you were so good with the girls. Erica misses you very much. I wish the last few months of your life would have been under better circumstances. I wish Bill and I would have known how bad life had gotten for you. That you thought you had to turn to drugs to feel better. I saw a side of you that I had never seen before, and I didn't like it. You know how your dad felt about drugs. He had no toleration for drugs. I also had lost my patience with you. I am glad we were able to get you into therapy and back on track. I hope that you really were turning your life around.

I go by where your accident was whenever I go to Emporia. I still have a hard time believing you're gone. The vehicle wasn't that bad that you should have died. If only you had your seatbelt on, I know you would still be here with us. I sometimes wonder if you prayed to God to take you; that life was just too hard for you. I hope you are at peace. Always know that we love you and miss you every day. We will never forget your easy-going ways, your big heart, and your beautiful smile. May God hold you and comfort you now, 'til we see each other again.

Love and miss you,

Jackie

P.S. I miss your hugs.

FROM: JACKIE MANWARING, STEPMOTHER

II

No Answer Why

Death is often difficult to accept,
impossible to understand.

MATTHEW SCOUT ADAIR

June 26, 1989 ~ November 15, 2010

He was the son of Jeff and Elaine Adair, and the brother of Benjamin.

He graduated from Seaman High School, Topeka, Kansas, and attended Kansas University. He worked at Kerry Foods in Gardner, Kansas. He enjoyed golf, music, and video games. He had a huge personality and the gift to make those around him laugh or smile. He was always available to help a friend day or night.

Matthew took his own life.

Dear Matthew,

Well, it is December again & time for my letter to you instead of
Santa. I can't believe it has been a year... Some things have changed
& other things will forever remain the same.

I wouldn't have believed it at this time last year, but things are better
— we are still broken & lost on the inside but we are able to function
& look ok on the outside. I miss you more every day instead of less
— not only missing what was but also missing what should have been
— for you & for us. It is hard to see your friends move on with their
lives — I know they should & it is healthy for them & what you would
have wanted, but it is still hard to watch & see what you are missing
out on. Your friends have been wonderful to us all — especially to
Ben — but even to Dad & me. Phil & Betsy are amazing, but that
whole group has taken us in. I think it helps them to be around us &
helps us to be around them. Every one of them reminds me of you in
the same way.

My grief does not take over every minute like it did last year, but it
is a big part of my day. I think it always will be. I feel so cheated —
you had so much to offer the world & other people — you were the
biggest personality I know. I loved being around you & spending time
with you & the older you got, the more I enjoyed you!

I can't imagine how much pain you must have been in to have left all
of us — mostly your friends. By being around them so much more, I
have a better understanding of how much you cared for them & how
much they loved you. In my darkest moments I am haunted by the
thought of your pain & how alone you must have felt, even though
you were surrounded by so much love. I cannot express how much I
wish you would have reached out to someone or diverted your atten-
tion or done anything to get through that moment & however many
more moments it took to get past the pain. We loved you uncondi-
tionally & even though you thought we were disappointed in you, we
would have helped you find your way.

I know you are in a better place & not in pain anymore & I am truly happy for that. I continue to talk to you & write to you all the time & at times have felt your presence & feel so blessed by that. I know you have a lot of people to watch out for… but keep close to us, Matty — we miss you so much & there are still times I don't know how I am going to get through the day without you. Watch over your brother & keep him safe — he is such an amazing kid & I am so sad that he won't be finishing his growing up with you around. You would be so proud of him — he is a lot like you but also his own person — the perfect combination. I hear you in his voice or laugh sometimes & I can't help but smile — it is a sad smile, but a smile nonetheless.

I love you & miss you more than words can express… to the moon & the stars. Every day I try to honor your life & your memory in some way. Love you, Matty!

Love, Mom

FROM: ELAINE ADAIR, MOTHER

RACHAEL RENEÉ CHAN

RACHAEL RENEÉ CHAN

December 28, 1973 ~ March 17, 1992

She was the daughter of Gary and Susan Chan, and the sister of Jeffrey.

She was a senior at Topeka West High School, Topeka, Kansas, where she would have graduated with honors. She worked at Chick-fil-A. She loved writing poetry, drawing, and painting. She was the art editor of the 1992 issue of "Calliope," the literary magazine of Topeka West. She collected teddy bears, volunteered with her explorer post at the Topeka Zoo, and was passionate about the environment.

Rachael died in a motorcycle accident.

Dear Rachael,

You were our "almost Christmas baby" born just three days later —
our little tax deduction. It gave us such pleasure watching you and
your brother Jeff growing up into caring and generous young adults.
We felt we were very fortunate to have been able to spend a lot of
time with you both and we have especially fond memories of the
many hours we volunteered at the Topeka Zoo helping out with
special events and the hand-rearing of the baby orangutans, Joseph
and Rudy.

You were initially a very shy young girl, but underneath that there
was a determination and what one might even call a "stubborn
streak" that served you well as you took on the challenges of life.
While you were always willing to listen to and consider the opinions
and advice of others, you were very much your own person, commit-
ted to the ideas and values you felt important.

Your passion for the arts was one of the characteristics that defined
you. You were so creative in your artwork and we are forever thankful for the beautiful drawings and paintings you left behind that now
grace the walls of our home. We often wonder where your love of
art might have taken you — would it have been a career path or a
lifelong hobby? Your poetry spoke of the human condition and the
emotions that come with simply being human. Your poems reflected
your view of life and the emotional challenges of anger, tolerance,
forgiveness, honesty and love.

Many of your formative years were spent as a member of the
Topeka Zoo Explorer Post. Most of the people you met and worked
with were older than you and this experience gave you a maturity
beyond your years. We also remember how the school trip to Europe
impacted your view of the world and broadened your appreciation
for other cultures. This too was a maturing experience for you.

Rachael, one of the things we will always remember about you
is your belief in the dignity of each and every life; how you truly
believed that people should "Just Take Life One Person at a Time."
We had bumper stickers made of your slogan and they adorn cars

in a number of states. We didn't know of all of your friends (you could also be a private person) nor did we realize the impact your death had on so many lives.

While we would do anything to make things different and for you to be here with us once again, we know that isn't possible. But what we have come to understand is that we honor your memory and your life best by living our own lives in meaningful and positive ways. It is easy to dwell on the many things we "lost" with your untimely death, but we feel it is also important for us to acknowledge and appreciate the many "gifts" you left behind for us.

We thank you for leaving us the following as a testament to your life and your love:

~ The gift of surprise and wonder that we think sometimes got lost when we were so busy trying to be good spouses, parents, employees, scout leaders, softball coaches, etc.

~ The courage to try and truly "Just Take Life One Person at a Time." We thank you for helping us see the good in everyone and not judge them with our preconceived notions. Your open and generous nature made us more willing to be accepting and open with people.

~ The ability to learn that not everything is as important or serious as we tended to think and that the world will go on just fine if we can't accomplish every goal we set for ourselves.

~ You reinforced our need to help others as a way of helping ourselves grow as people and, now, ultimately to heal.

~ Losing you has made us have a more heightened appreciation of life and a more reasonable view of what is truly important.

~ Your death has made us realize that we should not put off saying what we need to say to people — especially "I love you," "Thank you," and "I'm sorry."

~ Having you for a daughter gave us reason, despite so many terrible things happening in the world, to have hope for the future — because we know there are others like you out there trying to make things better.

~ Thank you for reminding us that there is much goodness in the world that we feel we often overlooked.

~ Thank you for making us realize that we mustn't get too busy making a living that we forget to make a life. You were right — making a living is what you get, making a life is what you give.

It is difficult most times for us to believe that you have been gone for over 20 years. We continue to miss, remember and love you every day with every heartbeat. While we treasure the many wonderful memories we have of you, we also grieve for "what might have been" — all the possibilities that life held for you, all the opportunities and experiences that you will never get to have. While we have come to accept that we cannot change what has happened, we still sometimes struggle with the unfairness of it all and the unanswerable question "WHY?"

With your death, our lives have turned out very differently than what we thought they might have been. But we also know that what you would want for us are lives well lived, with purpose, meaning and fulfillment. And so we must try and do our best to make you proud of us, Rachael, as we were always proud of you. We carry your love within our hearts. We miss you, Sweetheart. In love, you are remembered. In memory, you live.

Holding you in our hearts — now and always,

Mom and Dad

From: Susan and Gary Chan, mother and father

PAMELA KAY MCMASTER

August 12, 1957 ~ May 15, 2008

She was the daughter of Bennie and Alice McMaster, and the sister of Donald and Angela.

She graduated from Holton High School, Holton, Kansas, and Penn Foster College. She worked as a CMA at Holton Manor, Jackson County Nursing Home and the V.A. Hospital. She was devoted to her three children, Matt, Cissy, and Sally, as well as grandchildren, Stephanie, Micheal (both of whom she adopted), Ben, Bethany, and Christine.

Pamela was murdered.

My dearest Pam,

I will never forget the night I found out that you had been tragically
taken from me. It was May 15, 2008. I was watching the 10 o'clock
news on Channel 13. They said a woman had been shot outside her
motel room, which were used as apartments. I had a feeling it was
you. I called your sister, Angie, and she said, "No, mom, it couldn't
be Pam." A few minutes later, Sally (her daughter) called me and
said, "Grandma, I think it was Mom." I immediately called Angie
back and she came right away to me. We headed to the hospital,
Ang said, "Mom, what hospital?" I told her I didn't know. She got on
her cell and called Stormont-Vail and said, "I understand my sister
was involved in a shooting and I need to know if she is there?" They
asked her what her sister's name was and she said Pam McMaster
and they said, "Yes, she was there." She told them we were on our
way. When we arrived, they would not let us see you. We had to fill
out paperwork first. After that, they took us into a little room, off the
ER, to wait. Finally, after what seemed like an eternity, a detective
and a social worker came in and told you had been shot and did
not survive. My heart sank. I was devastated. I asked to see you, but
they would not let me, they said I could destroy evidence. I wanted to
tell you how much I love you. You were taken to the morgue for an
autopsy and then to the funeral home. You died on Thursday and I
didn't get to see you until Sunday. I asked Chris at the funeral home
if I could see you and he said he would not recommend it.

So, Honey, even though I didn't get to see you before you died, I
love you very much. I miss not having you around for the holidays,
birthdays and every other day. You always seemed to light up a room.
When you and your sister got together, lord knows something funny
was going to happen. Angie misses you and loves you very much.
Bethany and Christine used to ask me when Momo was coming
home. They still talk about you. Your memory is still in our hearts
and will be forever. You were always a kind and loving person that
would help anyone. When I found out that was just 15 minutes before you were shot, a little neighbor girl came over and told you she

was hungry. You fed her then sent her home. She was so upset over what happened to you. She drew a picture of an angel and placed it beside a lit candle in the spot you were shot.

Honey, I love you very much and miss you dearly.

All my love,

Mom

FROM: ALICE McMASTER, MOTHER

Dear Sis,

I will never forget the fateful day we lost you. It was a typical Thursday. I went over to Mom's that evening to check on her. I wanted to go see you, because I hadn't seen you since the Thursday before, it was around seven in the evening, but something was telling me not to. Around 7:30, again, I thought, "We really need to go see Pam," but something told me not to. I guess my guardian angel was trying to protect me. Normally, it would have taken me about 20 minutes to get there, which would have put us there around 7:40, the time you were shot to death.

I left Mom's and went home. It had only been about a half hour, Mom called and said, "I was watching the 10 o'clock news, that a woman was shot and killed at the motel and it looked like it was by Pam and Mike's room. I think it was Pam." I told her it couldn't be you. Why would anyone hurt you? A short time later, another call from Mom, "Ang, I'm pretty sure it was Pam that was shot." I went and picked Mom up and we headed to the hospital. I asked her what hospital? Mom didn't know. I called Stormont first and asked if she was there and they said yes. At the time, we had no idea, if, in fact it was you, because we hadn't received any notification from law enforcement.

When we get to the hospital, they wouldn't tell us anything about your condition. They wanted us to fill out our paperwork first. Then we were taken to a little room off the ER to wait. It was the same room you and I waited in when Mom had her heart attack. I knew it couldn't be good. After what seemed like an eternity a detective and a couple of other people came in and told us the news. All they could tell us was that you had been shot and died. They couldn't answer any questions because they were investigating. They refused to let us see you, because it could contaminate evidence. I was devastated. We were so close, enjoyed the same things. We had the bond that only sisters have. When we were growing up, we didn't have a lot of money and we were raised to appreciate the little things in life. We always had fun together working on florals, crafts, decorating and especially decorating Mom and Dad's old house for the holidays. We both loved Christmas. We worked together along with Mom, to take care of Dad when he was dying with cancer. I don't know how you did it, but you were working two jobs, taking care of Dad and raising a family on your own. We worked together to take care of Mom after she had her heart attack.

I didn't know how I was going to go on without you, to talk to, turn to when I needed you or do the things we enjoyed together. It would never be the same. You were the kindest person. You were great with the elderly patients that you walked with, even though you didn't have much, you were always willing to help someone in need.

I just don't understand why anyone would kill an innocent person they do not know in cold blood. How could you walk up behind someone and put four bullets in their back? Who was it? Why did they do it? Were they coming after us? This cold-blooded killer was roaming the streets of Topeka. We stayed close to home, almost afraid to go outside, watching anyone and everything around us.

I know you are in a better place. You're with Dad and the twins, watching over all of us. But losing you the way we did, that kind of pain never goes away. It's different when someone dies naturally, due to an accident or illness, but murder, is a different ball of wax. Lucky for us the person responsible was arrested within the first 48 hours. We spent a lot of time talking to detectives. Then there are all the legal issues, court, trial, sentencing. We had to sit about five feet away from the man that murdered you, during the trial, talk about trying. Mom and I were at every hearing, court appointment and everything else. When you have to sit in a courtroom and hear evidence, that you were not aware of, is beyond words. That's how we found out how many times you were shot, where you were shot, how the bullets traveled through your body, that you were sitting in a lawn chair out-side your room with your back to the shooter. You never even knew he was there. The details can be quite graphic, right down to the color of your undergarments and photos of the scene. The shooter received 25 years to life, which means he will be eligible for parole in 25 years. Then there will be parole hearings, it never goes away.

I spent a lot of sleepless nights. I couldn't sleep for any length of time. I could get up and go outside and sit for hours in the middle of the night. I know God would not let you suffer, that is my only consultation. I miss you dearly and I think of you every day, several times a day. I know one day we will all be together again, but for now, we have to suffer through the grief and anger of the situation.
It really hurts to see the other women doing things with their sisters and knowing I will never be able to do that ever again while I am on this earth.

I love and miss you, Sis.

All my love,

Ang

FROM: ANGELA ("ANGIE" MCMASTER) CARLSON, SISTER

STEVEN RUSSELL POWELL

May 21, 1991 ~ February 18, 2012

He was the son of Scott and Jean Powell, and brother of Crystal, Alisha, Sammi, and Christopher.

He graduated from Seaman High School, Topeka, Kansas, and Washburn Technical College, Topeka, Kansas. He worked for Midas as a mechanic and Life Patterns, where he worked with a mentally handicapped young boy.
His passion was working on cars. In high school he ran cross-country.

Steven took his own life.

Dear Steven,

I hurt, my head, my heart, my spirit, my soul. I don't know what
to do. I don't know how to live like this. I can't comprehend never
touching you again. No hugs. No kisses. No more laughter together.
I'll never hear your voice again. I'm going to forget the sound of
your voice. I'm so scared. I'm scared for your brother and sisters.
I'm scared I can't protect them. I cry and cry because I don't know
what else to do. I don't want to be this person. I don't want to understand the pain of losing a child. I should have done a better job.
I should have known things weren't right. What have I done for you
not to be able to confide in me? Why did you think you had the right
to just leave us! Leave us in such suffocating pain. I guess we need
you more than you needed us. I don't know and I'll never know. Yet
I'm supposed to find a way to make peace with that. I can't see that
happening. People say you're my angel now, looking out for me. I
don't need an angel, I need my son. Your dad needs his son and your
siblings need their brother, but you took that all away. And we're left
here to try to keep going on without you.

I do pray that you now have found peace and happiness. That is
all I've ever wanted for you. I just wish that could have happened
while surrounded by the people that love you and I'll always love my
beautiful boy, Steven.

Love,

Mom

FROM: JEAN POWELL, MOTHER

ADAM JAMES REAMS

November 24, 1989 ~ January 23, 2012

He was the son of Gene and Sandy Reams, and the brother of Nick. The family lived in Topeka, Kansas, after moving from Iowa in 1997.

He graduated from Shawnee Heights High School and attended Pittsburg State, Kansas State and Washburn universities. He was proud to be a member of the Navy ROTC. He loved the outdoors and cars. He played sports and was a huge fan of the San Francisco 49ers.

Adam had a lot of friends, but none as close as his brother, Nick.

Adam took his own life.

Our dearest Adam,

Instead of writing this letter, I really wish you were here with me,
with us. No words that I can write will explain or express how we feel,
or what life is now like, or take your place here with us. It's still unbelievable that you are gone. Someone commented that it had been 6
months, and I couldn't really comprehend and thought, "6 months?"
Or now, it's been 39 weeks. Even though I count the weeks and the
days, I often feel like I'm back in January, and you will come home.

I wish so much that right now, you were in your room, I could lie on
your bed and we could talk. But now when I lie on your bed, I cry
and miss you so much. But I talk to you every day, and sometimes
I just know what you would say, or see you smiling at me, your eyes
twinkling.

When the cops came to the door and told us you completed suicide
— the shock of it. None of us will ever forget that night. They had to
be wrong — you weren't a person who would do that. I waited then,
as I do now, for you to come home. I try to focus on the fact that in
death, as in life, you helped so many others. But this journey is unlike
any other because a parent should never outlive their child. I hope
you know how much I love you and how proud I am of you, but,
sometimes, I wonder when you left that night, did you hear me say,
"I love you?"

I believe you didn't want to go, but at that moment, for you, there
was no choice. I hope you felt our love, but sometimes I wonder,
given how busy life was, did you think I didn't care? I know, through
their grief some people have commented that you took the "easy way
out" or been angry with you. I don't know how they can say that or
be angry. What could be easy about the pain and despair or hope-
lessness you felt? I can't be mad at you for those feelings and I know
you didn't do this to hurt us. But, who or what is to blame? Sometimes, I feel anger towards the police for treating the call for help as a
crime call, or at the others involved that night. Sometimes, I am just
angry with myself. As your mom, shouldn't I have seen something or

known? Then I think of the events of the last day, and think, "Adam didn't know this would be the result, how could I?" And sometimes, I am so angry with God and question my faith and the meaning of life. How could this be God's plan, to take away not only my child, but your dad's son, Nick's brother and best friend? Why would God take someone who touched so many hundreds of lives with his caring, humor, help, love, and laughter?

But I know you will always be with me — sometimes, I feel your presence, your arms around me, or visiting me in dreams and memories. I am learning to find comfort in the fact that I am the proud mother of two sons that are/were not only brothers, but best friends. I will never forget you two often referring to yourselves as twins — completing each other's sentences, encouraging each other, steering each along in the course of life. I am learning to smile at these memories and in the fact that while you are not physically here, you are always with us — in our minds, our hearts, our souls. We talk about you, and to you, every day. Some people wonder why, but that is so easy — you are a part of each of us and our family. You and I were so alike — you often did many things that I did in my youth, like write poems.

So, here is my poem to you, my Adam:

> When people see me cry, they ask, "Why?"
> Was it something someone said, a memory, or event?
> They try, but can't understand what the loss
> > of our Adam has meant.
> Then someone asks, "How is your day?"
> And, I smile, and say, "OK."
> But to them, I'd really like to say:
> > tomorrow is just another day.

When I awake I must face
That my son, my Adam, is no longer in this place
No, instead, I must do what is expected of me
Regardless of how heavy or broken my heart may be.
Suicide, they whisper, is how you died —
         they don't know how hard you tried.
They whisper because they think there is shame,
         but I will always proudly speak your name.
I know now how dark and lonely
         depression and grief can be
And how those feelings took you away from me
See, I often feel that way inside
         and wish . . . that I had died.

Though they ask, they don't want to hear
         that I'd give my life to keep you here.
I miss your smile, your jokes, your laughter
All I have are memories until we meet again —
         in the world hereafter.
Yes, life goes on, with our broken dreams
But we love and miss you, Mr. Adam James Reams!
And I think of the families facing this same pain
And want to tell them, "Do what you must to stay sane."
Because the loss of a child is like no other,
Whether you are a sibling, father, or mother.

FROM: SANDY REAMS, MOTHER

III

BEYOND MEDICINE

*Science cannot provide all of the answers,
and disease does not play fair.*

MADISON HALEY ARNOLD

October 1, 1994 ~ March 12, 2009

She was the daughter of Tony and Susan Arnold, and sister of Mallory and Gaston.

She attended Indian Springs Middle School, Keller, Texas, and was looking forward to high school. She had many friends. She did not conform to any style but rather did her own thing. Her favorite color was orange. There is a statue in her honor at Madison's Walkway to Remember, and you can find more information at www.madasin.com

Madison died from complications due to leukemia.

My Madison,

I miss you beyond words. I talk to you often and wonder if you hear
me? I still can't believe you're gone. Everything happened so quick.
I wish those last 12 hours I could do all over again. When we were
at the doctor's office and I felt something wasn't right. I didn't want
to scare you, but kept asking the nurse are you sure everything is
ok? The nurse kept saying she's fine, mom. Quit worrying. When
the rude doctor asked you, "Are you always this cold?" When they
couldn't get your blood pressure. So many things and they didn't see
you were dying. I'm so sorry. You were always so brave and never
complained, ever. I wish you had. Maybe you were just too brave.
I have no idea what your last hours were like. I just pray you were
not in pain. I hope you were in a state that you didn't know you were
dying. I hope you weren't afraid. It haunts me, and I know it haunts
your dad. I was supposed to protect you. Make sure everything was
OK. You trusted me above all others to take care of you. I did everything I could to make sure you were taken care of, but it still wasn't
enough because you're gone.

I always had a premonition that I would die before 14. When I
passed that age I thought there was something wrong with me. That
premonition was right. However it wasn't me, it was you. When you
died part of me died with you. It's an everyday struggle to carry on
without you. We see many signs you are still around. Please keep
sending those our way. I want you to know you are the first thought I
have when I wake and the last thought I have when I go to sleep and
thousands of thoughts in between.

Life is unfair. It is unfathomable we must continue our life without
you. We talk of you often and we feel you are around. I live on faith
that we will see you again. If we didn't have that, life would seem
senseless. I know we have to struggle our remaining days without you,
but I also know that when we see you again it will be the happiest
moment of our lives and all those years without you will not matter,
because we will be together again. I just will miss so many moments.
Your high school years, graduation, college, your wedding and your
children. Your brother and sister will miss having you in their lives

and it will be a great loss not having you be the great fun aunt that you would have been.

We just miss you more than words can say. I miss your funny personality, your sweet nature, I miss your voice calling out for me and I miss your hugs. You had the best hugs. When I really need you and it seems unbearable I can actually feel you give me a hug. I can actually still feel them. It gives me great comfort and I can't thank you enough for that.

We miss you every second of every minute of every hour of every day!

Love you & always missing my Madison

Mom

FROM: SUSAN GASSO ARNOLD, MOTHER

JOE MARLIN GREEN

August 2, 1954 ~ September 16, 1999

Son of Earl Green and Louise Johnson, and brother of Larry and Roberta.

He attended Highland Park High School, Topeka, Kansas. He then joined the United States Army. He worked as a self-employed truck driver. Father of Mindy Jo, grandfather of twins Hailey and Heather. He loved to cook and made wonderful fried fish. He also loved hunting and fishing.

Joe died from a heart attack.

Dearest Son Joe,

Well want to tell you what has been going on since you passed away Sept. 16th, 1999.

Your daughter, Mindy Jo, had twin girls. Their names are Hailey & Heather. Your brother Larry Green & sister Roberta Green miss you very much. Larry misses you going hunting with him. Your sister misses you very much, always wants to talk about you. The place where she goes in the daytime tells her, "You don't need to talk about it, that you're in a good place with Jesus." That is what I tell her also.

Your niece Stephanie got married to Norman Clark and they have two boys and two girls. Niece Ashley got married to Kurt Paugh and have one daughter, Ryleigh Marie Paugh.

Mom misses you very much. I enjoyed your cooking & your fried fish.

Also your sister asks, "When will I see Jody?" I'll say when we die and go to heaven. I'm praying you're in heaven. But we won't know if you're not there, that's what the Bible tells us.

You have and we all have missed a lot without you.

Mom will always love you and miss you till I die.

I've had a lot of hard times, but God, has been good to me and I love the Lord with all my heart and soul.

Love & Prayers

Your Mom

From: Louise Johnson, mother

JEAN ANN IRISH

November 19, 1955 ~ December 1, 2010

She was the daughter of Betty Wagner.

She graduated from Highland Park High School, Topeka, Kansas. She worked for Shawnee County Parks and Recreation. She loved cooking, going to church and spending time with her family. She had daughters, Tracey and Becky.

Jean died from pancreatic cancer.

Dearest Momma,

First of all I want to say how much I miss you and how much I wish you were here. I will never forget that day you called me at work and said the doctor said you might have cancer but not to worry and trust in God and everything would be OK. It wasn't. Pregnant with my son at the time I could barely grasp what I was going to be going through. You were so excited I was pregnant. I tried to believe in what you said and trust in God. You had stage IV pancreatic cancer. Why did this have to happen to such a caring and loving person?? It's not fair, Momma. My heart broke when they told me you only had six months to live, come to find out you were gone in two months, Mom. I never told you how much I loved you and how much you meant to me and what a wonderful mother you were to me. I will never be the same without you in my life, Mom. You would have been such a wonderful grandmother to my son. You told me when you were sick that God does everything for a reason and at that moment I knew God gave me my special angel baby body because he had bigger plans for you and he needed you. Marley gives me the strength to keep going on each day when I don't think I can take anymore. You would have been so proud of him, Momma. He is so special to me and I know he would have been special to you also. I would do anything if I could have one more day with you and you could meet him.

Momma I will never forget you and you will always hold a special place in my heart!! They say God only takes the best, and I know you are the best!!! For you have other work to do, Momma. I love you so much and I want to thank you for everything you did for us and for the memories we made when you were here. Until we meet again, Momma. I LOVE YOU AND MISS YOU!! You're my angel!!!!

Love Always,

Tracey, Aaron and Marley

FROM: TRACEY MALONE, DAUGHTER

HEATHER KRISTIN LEONARDI

September 8, 1988 ~ March 31, 2001

She was the daughter of Glen Leonardi and Jefri Franks.

She enjoyed hunting, fishing, reading, drawing, writing, swimming, and spending time with her group of six girl-friends. She loved to learn and enjoyed school. She loved her cat (Rachel) and her dogs named (Katie and Hanna). She wanted to be a veterinarian or an architect when she grew up.

Heather died from cancer.

My Dearest Angel,

It is hard to pick just one way to address you, there are so many. Boo
Boo Girl, DeeDoo, Rackoo Shakoo Kakoo, Gweeka, Mommy's Girl,
Exquisite Creature ... to name a few. You are the best thing to ever
happen to me. You brought me my motherhood which I now know
is eternal. I still feel like a mom, your mom, even though you are
no longer on earth with me. When I am fortunate enough to inter-
act with a young girl, I feel those "mom muscles" come alive again!
There is a brand new baby girl across the street. Robert and I are on
the babysitting list — I know this makes you as happy as it makes me.

When you were first born, I realized how frighteningly vulnerable
I was. I had always believed that I could survive anything this world
could throw me ... until you. I did not see a survival scenario for me
if something were to happen to you. I didn't know there was a love
this deep, this precious. You took my breath away. You stripped me
of all my defenses. When you were diagnosed with cancer in 2000
I experienced my own personal Y2K. I was brought to my knees.
It was there, on my knees one night at Children's Mercy Hospital
that I saw my mistake. I had always thought that whatever I wanted,
I could make it so. Whatever I didn't want to happen, I could stop.
I realized then that I have no control over what life may bring me. I
can only control how I decide to respond.

I will be forever grateful for the last 11 months we spent together
before you died. We were joined at the hip — you and me against
the world, against the horrid disease. Through it all we held hands
as you deployed your wicked sense of humor, your kindness, your
compassion, your bravery. We faced it all with our eyes wide open

and our ragged hearts on fire. One day you asked for my permission to leave and with God's help, I gave it to you. I told you I was not going to say goodbye because we would be seeing each other again in heaven. A few days later you took your last breath with your dad and I holding your hands. We died that day, too. Somehow we drove home and began the long, slow climb out of the sub-basement of hell.

Your wonders didn't cease when you left this earth. You worked so hard to show me, tell me that you indeed were alive and well in the Heavenly Kingdom. I remember the night you appeared to me. The many times you sent a sentence through my head. The many family members and friends who also experienced you, calling me, breathless with the good news. Thank you for working so very hard to reassure all of us who love you so much that what we have been told about God and heaven is true.

Not a day goes by that I don't think of you. You were worth all of the despair, anguish and agony. I thank God for lending a piece of your precious soul to me for 12 awesome years. Although there is more for me to do on earth I am so excited to reunite with you in the Kingdom! I especially love when you visit me in my dreams and we just hold hands and talk — as though cancer had never touched our lives. Because of you I know that love never dies. Our relationship, though drastically changed, continues on. Because of you and God and all of the help you have given me, I am able to reach out to other grieving souls and offer hope. Thank you for being my daughter!

All my mommy love for eternity,

Your mom, MeeDoo

FROM: JEFRI LEONARDI FRANKS, MOTHER

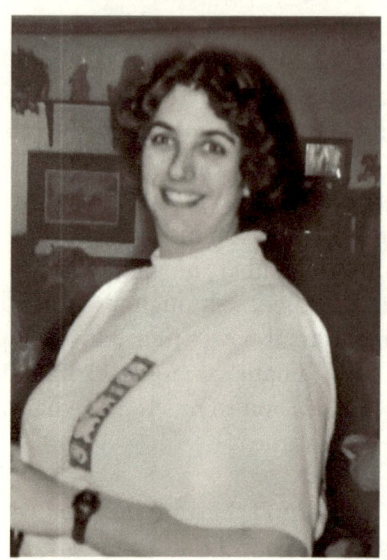

EMILY JANE "JANIE" SCHROEDER

July 30, 1961 ~ March 25, 2008

She was the daughter of Richard Schroeder and Marilyn Schroeder, sister of Katherine, David, Dan, and Tommy (deceased).

She graduated from Raytown High School, Raytown, Missouri, and Longview Junior College, Kansas City, Missouri. She worked several jobs and took great pride in her work. She had one daughter, Christa. She loved animals of all kinds especially cats and her beloved horse, Cherokee. She loved visiting antique shops with her mother. She loved yard work, was an excellent cook and a wonderful friend.

Janie died from breast cancer.

Dear Janie,

How I miss your cheerful "hello" in our almost daily phone calls.
The devotion we shared was one of the most special things in my
life. You were always game to go along with me on thrift store
and antique store junkets; trips out to Denver to see your beloved
brothers, David and Dan; musical and dramatic events; or just out to
eat. It was so much fun to work with you on painting rooms in your
darling little house. You took such pride in maintaining your home.

Your unfailing kindness was amazing to experience. I think you
seldom, if ever, had an unkind thought for anyone in your life.
This is the quality you possessed that is most often noted by others.

Your bravery in the face of dealing with a terrible illness as your
cancer metastasized from breast to bones, brain, and lungs was an
inspiration to behold.

At the end, you were tired and ready to go. You had faith that you
would be in heaven. You were always my angel.

Love,

Mom

FROM: MARILYN SCHROEDER, MOTHER

THOMAS HEIM SCHROEDER

September 14, 1970 ~ March 23, 2002

He was the son of Richard Schroeder and Marilyn Schroeder, brother of Janie (deceased), Katherine, David, and Dan.

He graduated from Lawrence High School, Lawrence, Kansas, and The University of Kansas. He worked for Kaw Valley Engineering. He loved music and played trumpet in the KU marching band. He was in the process of learning the banjo. He was married to Marci, and they had one daughter, Erica, born just 10 weeks before his passing. He was wise beyond his years, with a quick wit, an infectious laugh, and a generous spirit.

Thomas died from colon cancer.

Dear Tom,

I think of you so often — like the words of Willie Nelson's song, "You are always on my mind." All my memories of you are good ones. How I loved your quick wit, your capable nature, and your emotional strength. You were always there for both your dad and me, willing to do things for us if we needed your help. You made me proud to have you as a son.

You would be so happy if you would see how your daughter, Erica, is flowering. She is a beautiful 10-year-old now. She takes dancing lessons and has been in several recitals. She is a straight-A student, loves school, and is already showing both musical and artistic talents. She looks like both you and Marci. And Marci tells me that she is very much like you in many ways.

As you would suppose, Marci is a fabulous mother. She has given Erica a stable and loving upbringing and I know Erica feels secure. Erica's Aunt Jackie and Grandma Jo are an important part of her life, too.

I don't know what to believe of the "afterlife," but your sister, Janie, was a strong believer. And before her death four years ago, she said to her dad, "What shall I tell Tommy?" I hope you are together in some way. You made a large impact in your too short life and you are remembered.

Love,

Mom

FROM: MARILYN SCHROEDER, MOTHER

UNBORN BABY GIRL ASHBY

November 13, 1991 (d.)

Carla Ashby lost her baby November 13, 1991.

She never had any other children.

As I sit and write this birthday wish, the words I want to say seem to come very slowly. Bit by bit, little by little, the ink unhurried to leave the pen and the words gently and deliberately landing on the page.

I stop to think of all the things a child goes through on their journey to grow up. All the laughter and all the joys; all the pain and all the tears; all the wishes and all the dreams; all the experiences they might have had.

There's nothing more wonderful than the sound of a child's laughter. There's nothing more tragic than a child's tears. There's nothing more exciting than a child's adventures.

It would be easy to remember only the good things that happen in a child's life. But to understand how a child grows requires that you remember every skinned knee, every friendship that fell apart, every fear that was calmed, every broken heart, and every frown that was overturned by a smile.

I wonder what events shape a child the most. Is it the safety they feel from a mother's hug? Is it the bravery they learn through a father's faith? Is it the thrill of a love's first kiss? Is it the excitement of one accomplishment? Or is it the triumph of a hundred small successes?

Twenty years is a long time to remember and even longer to wonder. Wonder how you would have celebrated this birthday. Wonder how many of the joys, tears, and accomplishments you might have had. Wonder if you might have played guitar. Wonder if you would have loved to learn. Wonder if you might have traveled the world or stayed right here at home.

I remembered you growing up in the hopes and dreams I had for you. I remember again and again each day of the life you might have had.

I wish for you a Happy Birthday; a happy birthday to my child that was never born.

Mom

FROM: CARLA ASHBY, MOTHER

Julie Ann Westoff

October 16, 1966 ~ December 26, 2013

Julie was the daughter of Earl and Carolyn Westhoff and sister of Paul Westhoff, Debra Dodd and Steve Westhoff. Julie was preceded in death by her mother Carolyn Westhoff.

Julie,

It's painful writing to you. It makes it feel real. I still like to pretend
we will be seeing each other soon. I feel that you hear my thoughts. I
almost always have an idea of what you would say back. You're often
a voice in my head telling me to be a little fancier. You saw people
for who they were, good or bad. I like to think everyone is good, just
having a bad day.

As I've gotten older, I laugh when I remember you telling me how
smiling "that much and that big" will cause wrinkles. I would just
laugh and then you would laugh too.

I have so many memories of us. Memories as roommates in Houston and in Kansas City. Memories of us driving from KC to Denver,
Denver to Scottsdale, Scottsdale to Houston, San Diego, and Glamis.
Memories at family weddings in St. Louis, Palm Springs, and Kansas.
Memories from when we were young and as adults, always having
fun and laughing until the sun came up. I'll never forget when we
met in San Diego at Cami's. She wanted to see my return ticket to
make sure we were actually planning on going home. Memories from
our trip to Hawaii where I thought we would find a cure for cancer.
You looked so beautiful there. I didn't want to believe how sick you
were.

I remember you saying that people would remember you for a while,
then they would forget and move on. You said it just works that way.
Well, no one that has ever met you has forgotten you. You were such
a vibrant, smart, dramatic, lover of football (and the players), creative, opinionated, beautiful girl. You are remembered and missed
every day. I often quote things you would say and take your advice.
If you don't have good perfume with you, a good smelling hair spray
will work. Mackenzie still uses your dating advice.

The world seemed safer when you were here. I was able to trust you. You were honest. Really honest.

I know there were times when it was hard to see me get excited about little things, like butterflies and playing with Hayden, while you were in so much pain. I didn't know what to do. I didn't know how to fix it. I couldn't even think about your physical and emotional pain. It hurt. I was in disbelief.

I couldn't ever say goodbye and that I would miss you in a way that felt like it could be the last time. It was just too hard. I think you wanted me to. I really tried.

I still can't say goodbye.

I miss and love you, Julie,

Marti

FROM: MARTI HILL, COUSIN

IV

WITHOUT WARNING

*When lives are whisked away in the blink of an eye,
there is only pain to fill the void.*

JASON WAYNE ALLDREDGE

April 30, 1982 ~ April 24, 2002

He was the son of Stan Alldredge and Sue Alldredge, and the brother of Andy.

He graduated from Free State High School in Lawrence, Kansas, and was attending Wyoming Tech at the time of his passing. He loved working on cars and was always willing to help his many friends with their auto repair needs. He also loved to hunt and fish and enjoyed tying his own fishing flies.

Jason died in an auto accident.

Dear Jason,

I love you and I miss you.

It has been 10 years since you were taken from us and not a day goes by that I don't think of you and long to talk to you again. I miss my son and I miss my best friend.

When you were taken from our life, so many things changed for everybody that knew and loved you.

I lost out on seeing you grow as an adult and succeed at life. I missed out on your children, my grandchildren.

Andy missed out on having his big brother around to help guide him.

Your friends all missed out on your humor and positive attitude to help us laugh at life.

I miss working on our projects together. They do not have the same joy as when you and I worked together.

There is still a hole in my heart from when you were taken.

I pray that there is a God and an afterlife, and that you are in a better place.

Your friends still keep in touch and try to help. That means a lot, to know that you are not forgotten by others. I watch them grow and progress in life and can only wonder why you were taken, and what you would have become.

I am so proud of you and your dedication to become the best at what you wanted for a career.

I am glad that we got to come out there and see you and tell you we love you the week before the accident that took you away from us.

Your mother and I grew apart after your death, I hope you are not disappointed in me for her and me getting divorced. We both love you very much and miss you.

I will finish rebuilding your truck the way you had planned, and Andy and I will take it to auto shows for you. I hope you are happy with us and our work.

I would happily trade places with you, and have you here on earth, enjoying your life and all of its promise, and died myself if one of us had to go. Too many people suffered too much hurt when children are taken so young.

We all have struggled with why you died and the driver walked away from the accident. You had so much promise and potential. You had a plan for your future and you were going after it.

I love you and I miss you, my son.

Dad

FROM: STAN ALLDREDGE, FATHER

BRIAN WAYNE ASHBURN

December 29, 1989 ~ May 9, 2002

He was the son of Susan Ashburn and Arlen Ashburn, and the brother of Beth and Nick.

He attended school in Reading, Kansas. He loved to play basketball, fish, camp, shoot clays, ride his go-cart, and ride horses. He won several buckles in team penning. He loved spending time with his best friend, Daniel Dieker. Brian was full of life, kind and considerate, and he is greatly missed.

Brian died in an accident at his home.

Dear Brian,

Although I did not give birth to you, I always considered you my son. When you died, a part of me died with you. People say it gets easier with time, but in all reality, time just goes by. Not a day has gone by that I don't think about you. I know that God blessed us with you here on earth for 12 short years, but I so wish it would have been longer. You gave us so much joy. I often share stories of you and Nick when you were small boys. Such great memories. Remember the fishing? Of course you do. Every time I go into Walmart, I think about walking in with my arms around you and Nick saying, "My two favorite boys," the music in the little truck, planting flowers, I could go on and on with all of the memories I hold near and dear to my heart. In the end of someone's life, all we have left are the memories. I am so thankful you gave me so many to cherish.

You leaving us left so many broken hearts, several are with you now. I know you welcomed Grandma and Grandpa and will welcome the rest of us when the time comes.

Much Love,

Aunt Pammy... you know ...
"Aunt Pammy #1, favorite and best! I love my Aunt Pammy and diamonds are a girl's best friend!"

FROM: PAM PURDUM, AUNT

JACOB BRADLEY "JAKE" BINFIELD

August 6, 1985 ~ January 27, 2011

He was the son of Brad and Jenny Binfield, and the brother of Sarah.

Jake graduated from Seaman High School and worked for the Union Pacific Railroad. He had many friends, drawn by his sense of humor and his smile. He always looked forward to two things in particular: game day for the Nebraska Cornhuskers and hunting trips with his uncles and cousins.

Jacob died of complications from a diving accident.

My Dear Jake,

I've thought of you so very much since you have been gone. It seems my days are spent thinking of every single thing about you so I won't forget. I guess at this point (1 year, 9 months, and 17 days) I'm afraid I will forget. I don't want to forget as it seems most others have.

It was hard to see you struggle with your paralysis. I wanted it to be me and not you. I would have taken your place. It was a huge loss for you. I look back on the last 5 years since your accident and it seems like such a long time ago but yet it seems like yesterday when I was helping you, going to the trail to exercise, stopping at Sonic for mozzarella sticks, chicken bites, and a drink. You worked so hard to move that chair and it paid off. The UPPERTONE, standing frame, therapy, surgery ....

Let's not forget the fighting, laughing, crying, and being pissed off about the whole deal either! It sucked! The most for you, Jake, but it sucked for all of us. But in the end love prevailed.

It seems so unfair that you had to go through all you did with that, only to have it end so suddenly. Done. No suffering any more. Which is what we all wanted for you but never thought of it in terms of you dying.

I cleaned the freezer out yesterday and found your fish you caught before your accident. All wrapped in newspaper just like the day you left it, waiting to be measured so it could be mounted. I loved fishing with you and cried this year when they opened the season for trout fishing. It was a beautiful day but I couldn't go without you.

I'm finding out there are a lot of things I miss about you. The way you walk, talk, tease, laugh, and the way you light up a room when you come in. I miss your music playing loud. The way you smell.

Most of all your smile. It would be well to say that I miss *everything* about you.

I usually struggle about a week before your birthday. Seems to be the same for holidays too. Everyone seems to think I am doing so well, they just don't see the tears, the sleepless nights, the lost look while roaming around the mall ... they just don't see. I guess they can't because they've never lost a child. I'm not angry at them for not understanding. I feel different now. Like I don't fit in with "normal" people.

Jake, here lately I've been needing someone to talk to: You know how we used to just complain about people and the other would validate the complaint?

How about the phone calls from North Platte?

And remember when you surprised me for Christmas? I was making cookies when you called to say you wish you could be home for Christmas but you had to work your new job. It was to be our first Christmas without you and you said, "Just a minute, someone is knocking at my door." And I said, "Hey, someone is knocking at my door, too!" ... I dropped the phone and ran to the door, it was you, home for Christmas! Every Christmas I get this strange feeling that you will be calling and coming home ...

I guess I'll end this letter for now. I really just wanted you to know how deeply you are missed and loved, even though you aren't here. I know I will see you again. Thanks for putting the X's in the sky ... I love you too!

XO
Mom

FROM: JENNY BINFIELD, MOTHER

RYAN EDWIN GUNTHER

October 15, 1983 ~ June 6, 2008

He was the son of Bruce Gunther and Tamah Boyce, and brother of Craig.

He graduated from Valley Falls High School, Valley Falls, Kansas. He worked at the K-Mart Distribution Center, Lawrence, Kansas. He had a deep love of humanity, music, the arts, and the outdoors.

Ryan died in an auto accident.

Ry,

I always thought the worst fear in life would be to have one of your children pass away. I always thought of how devastating it would be and how could the parents ever go on.

My worst nightmare came true on the evening of June 6, 2008. I wondered that night as I hugged your jackets hanging in the hall how will I, how will we be able to live without you.

Ryan, you and Craig are my life and my strength.

It's not easy to put into words all my emotions and memories flooding in my head and in my heart. There are so many.

I will start by thanking you for being such a great son, brother, grandson, godfather, nephew, cousin and friend to all. Everyone loved you. You showed compassion for every living thing in life, including setting insects free.

People would say you stood out from the crowd. You wouldn't have to say much, but you always touched people with your kind and gentle soul.

You always played a special beat to your own set of drums in life. I miss your smile and your deep, peaceful chuckle. I miss your unique sense of humor.

You and Craig would always have music in the air. If not on the radio, you'd be playing your drums and Craig would be on his guitar. You both were amazing in everything you did. You weren't only brothers, but true friends. From having a great fun sense of humor to being serious in your beliefs, having moral courage and when seeing a wrong to try to right it.

I have been blessed to have been your Mom.

How do I go on. It has been 4 ½ years. I am able to go on because of your strengths and your beliefs.

This is your 2012. You believed that it wasn't that the world would end, it was your hope that there would be a spiritual awareness and awakening. That there is more to life than people realize in their fast pace day in and day out.

I cherish the times you woke me up or called me to go out and look up at the sky at night. You would say, "Mom, you gotta go look at the moon and the stars, the sky looks really cool tonight."

My memory of that was yes, the moon and stars were awesome, but watching you beside me looking up at the glory of the heavens made it even more awesome for me.

Thank you for the sweet memories. I loved whenever I told you, "I love you, Ry," you would always say, "Likewise" & "Watch your back." You always looked out for me.

You always told me the #5 would go into play with you, but you didn't know why. Now we know.

Thank you for the signs from the #5 to dragonflies to all the other special signs you've given us along the way.

I truly believe that through your poem, paintings, our talks and your beliefs of spiritual awareness that you were preparing us that everything is going to be okay.

This is your 2012. Your year of hope.

With Von putting these loving pages together, I can see you smile and hear you say in your peaceful voice, "That's really cool."

You have touched so many lives in your 24 years and continue to do so and we thank you.

You are a very powerful soul.

I was told that the day of the accident you had Danny stop the car so you could pick a pink rose that was blooming on the side of the road and that you carried that rose around with you that day.

There is so many cherished memories that I will treasure in my heart, mind and soul forever.

We love you, Ry. Our thoughts and love are with you every day and I will promise you in life that I will take the time to stop and smell the roses.

Ma

FROM: TAMAH BOYCE, MOTHER

JONATHAN JEFFREY KASPAR

September 17, 1989 ~ June 4, 2010

He was the son of Jeffrey and Susan Kaspar, and the brother of Jennifer.

He graduated from Hayden High School, Topeka, Kansas, and was attending Washburn University. He worked as a barista at P.T.'s Coffee Company. He was a gifted writer and poet and was passionate about a variety of humanitarian causes. He loved soccer and a good cup of coffee. P.T.'s named the blend SOL in his honor.

Jonathan died in an auto accident.

Jonathan,

You are always with me. I see you in the morning sunrise, feel you in the gentle breeze, hear you when the birds sing, miss you with all my heart, love you with all my soul.

Love, Mom

Happy Birthday, Jonathan …

"Good morning, sunshine," I would say, as I kissed your curls and welcomed the day.

Then a great big hug, I held you tight, those moments now treasures, made the world just right.

"We have things to do and people to see, such a beautiful day, and it's you and me."

I watched you grow from a baby so sweet, to a bright little boy, soccer shoes on your feet.

The Giving Tree and *Goodnight Moon*, books scattered all over your room.

"We have things to do and people to see, such a beautiful day, and it's you and me."

You continued to grow into a charming young man, with a heart of gold, always lending a hand.

Bringing joy to others came so naturally, a true gift from God helping others to see,

"There are things to do and people to meet, slow down and take time, for just you and me."

Today I'll take time for you and me, though there are places to go and people to see.

Keeping you close in my heart through the day, rest well with the angels my wish as I pray,

May God hold you close and fill you with love, keeping you safe in heaven above.

I love you, Mom

FROM: SUSAN KASPAR, MOTHER

ANDREW LYLE MCLAREN

November 17, 1989 ~ November 1, 2006

He was the son of Greg and Amy McLaren, brother of Kristen.

He was a student at Washburn Rural High School, Topeka, Kansas. He played baseball and was a musician, performing with the Exaltation Ringers and the Washburn Rural Choral music program. He loved music. He loved to debate and was always making people laugh. He had a strong faith in God, and was a member of First Baptist Church. He had many friends and is greatly missed.

Andy died in an auto accident.

OF COURSE!

I don't know quite where to begin this letter, Andy. You've been gone over 5 years now, but it seems like yesterday. I see you in nearly everything from the sunrise and sunset to the golf course and baseball diamonds. I can't go into a hotel pool without remembering your antics with the bubble bath in the hot tub. Oh boy, you were a fun guy. I could always count on you to pick me up on a bad day and to push my buttons on a good day.

I guess this letter is more about memories than anything else. My strongest memories are of you casually walking into our bedroom after an evening out with your friends. You seemed to grow so tall in the last year. Your presence was huge. You just wanted to come in to talk or simply hang out. You seemed to enjoy being with us and were never embarrassed to be with your folks, like most teens.

I remember holding hands with you while driving in the car going places when you were young. You'd sit in the front seat with me, and we would simply hold hands — no words were necessary. It was fun watching you grow up and hold other girls' hands. I knew you'd make a wonderful boyfriend, husband and father someday.

The baseball diamonds were where I always felt most connected to you. We both had that competitive spirit. Whenever you were up on the pitching mound, I was so proud of you. Somehow I felt connected to you. Remember your no-hitter game in that tournament? Wow! Unbelievable!

I remember when you chose to give up soccer, which you were so talented at, in order to play football with your buddies. You just weren't big enough to play football, but that didn't deter your competitiveness. You gave it everything you had. I loved that about you.

You will be forever 16 in my memory, but now my fears are much different. I don't fear your decisions or your safety that all mothers worry about. My fear is now within myself that your memories remain fresh in my mind. I never want to forget your ornery smile, your gentle spirit, your loving ways. As I grow older I fear those memories will fade, and I will forget the sound of your voice or the warmth of your embrace. Even as I write this, my tears are falling. I miss you terribly.

Right now I am looking out over the Atlantic Ocean, and it's easy to see God's majesty before us. I have never doubted God's plan for our lives. Obviously there was a good reason God took you from this earth. I may never know the true reason. I pray that He can use me to help someone else in the same predicament. I do know two things for sure ... our reunion in Heaven will be the sweetest ever, and that the full reason for God's plan will be revealed. And I will have but two words ... "Of course!"

Love you, Andy Man!

Mom

FROM: AMY MCLAREN, MOTHER

Andy,

I miss your fastball and curveball. I miss your hitting one over the fence, or a hard hit line drive to center. I miss your running the bases, or turning a single into a double. I miss your encouraging your team-mates. Safe at Home

I miss what you would have become, where you would have gone to college, who you would have brought home. Safe at Home

I miss being with you at the ballgame, making sly remarks about the other team. All the statistics you could produce on a moment's notice. Safe at Home

I miss your smile at the dinner table, you helping around the house, and mowing the yard when it needed it. Safe at Home

I miss you becoming a man, and standing up for what you are for, and rejoicing with you as you grew with Jesus. Safe at Home

I miss all the times we could have been together. All the smiles and good times, I just miss you not being here. Safe at Home

One day I'm going to see you, you are going to greet me. I want to give you a big hug, and tell you face to face how much I love you. Safe at Home

Love, Dad

FROM: GREG MCLAREN, FATHER

JERRY KEVIN MURRAY

May 1, 1962 ~ July 19, 1979

He was the son of Gary and Sherry Murray, and the brother of Terry.

He was a student at Seaman High School, Topeka, Kansas. He worked at Culligan Water Softeners. He loved to work and had worked driving a dump truck for the county when he was only 16. His passion was motocross racing. He was very competitive and won often. He also liked to hunt and fish.

Jerry died in a car accident.

Dear Jerry,

This is what I would tell you if I had the chance to talk to you once
more. I didn't want our last talk to be in anger. I always wanted a
better life for you and Terry than I had. I didn't want you to come
from a broken home. I know what you told me the last time we talked
on the phone was true. I had known for some time, but my hands
were tied. I couldn't support you and Terry on my own, there was no
one I could ask for help. I was in the hospital at the time we talked.
Around midnight, I got out of bed and walked to the window. I felt
something was wrong, but had no idea what. I wanted to talk to you
and try to make you understand. I wanted you to know there was
nothing in the whole world that meant more to me than my boys.
I loved you both so much. I couldn't raise you on my salary. I know
your dad loved, you, too. But your dad hadn't grown up yet. He still
wanted the good times of a single person. I hope the truth about
all of this didn't make you want to do anything foolish. We all had
a hard time going on without you. We still do at times, but I know
nothing will ever bring you back. I only pray that someday we will be
together again and I can make you understand. But until then, life
goes on. I blame myself. Maybe if I had been at home instead of the
hospital, we could have talked face-to-face. I think back on your short
life. You were lucky, in some ways. You loved racing motorcycles and
you were good at it. You liked to fish and hunt with your dad. You
worked at summer jobs. You drove a dump truck for the county when
you were only 16. You worked at Culligan Water Softeners in the
evenings while you were going to school. Your friends said you lived
life to the fullest. I wanted so much more for you and Terry. I'm so
sorry. Until we meet again, I love you and miss you very much, and
I hope you are still riding on.

Love,

Mom

FROM: SHERRY MURRAY, MOTHER

DALTON LEE WESTPHAL

July 3, 1993 ~ August 22, 2009

He was the son of Darryl and Paula Westphal, and brother of Shawna.

He was a student at Shawnee Heights High School, Tecumseh, Kansas. He loved hunting, fishing, and sports. His favorite was soccer. He was a natural athlete and excelled at every level. He was very intelligent and was an honor student in school. He had an inquisitive nature and was always finding new ways to occupy his time. He never failed to bring a smile to those around him.

Dalton died in an auto accident.

WITHOUT YOU

Dalton,

Living my life without you here seems impossible right now. I just keep thinking you'll be sitting at the table doing homework or on the computer downloading music or watching some crazy YouTube video. Every morning I think I need to go wake you up. I figured I would be doing that until you went off to college. I still watch for school closings when it's cold and snowing out. I want to come tell you school is closed and you can sleep in. You will be so excited & then you'll call me later to tell me you're going to go 4-wheeling or sledding with friends.

When I stop myself and realize none of these things are ever going to happen again it, totally overwhelms me. It's like having my heart & soul ripped out. I can't seem to get past the crying, sadness, feelings I get. The tears will just start and I can't seem to turn them off.

I know you're supposed to let your feelings out, but it doesn't seem to make me feel any better. When I get done crying then I have a headache and can't concentrate or think about anything.

Life just seems to keep moving even though I don't want it to. All your friends are going on with high school, finding girlfriends, enjoying activities & growing up. Why can't you be here to do that with them?

I love you and miss you every day.

Mom

FROM: PAULA WESTPHAL, MOTHER

V

PARENTS & GRANDPARENTS

Our elders and teachers are missed,
even after lives lived long and well.

RAYMOND CLYDE ASHBY

May 15, 1924 ~ December 9, 1981

He was the son of Lindsey and Cora Ashby, and brother of Lee, Pat, Howard, Donald, and Vestanna.

He graduated from St. John High School, St. John, Kansas. He worked as a carpenter. He was an excellent guitar player and loved to paint. He married Shirley, and they were parents of Linda, Russell, Susan, Donna, Cheryl, David, Carla, and Karen.

Raymond died from a heart attack.

Dear Dad,

As I write this letter to you I realize that it has been more than 30 years since you passed away. I was just 20 years old when you died. Oh, how everything has changed since you were with us ...

Grandkids ... so many grandkids and now great grandkids. You had the great fortune to meet the first of many of them — Vestanna, Nathan, Chris and Brandon. You remember Adam didn't make it very long in this world, bless his little heart. I think that was the first great loss for our family. You were the next.

Now you have so many grandkids and great grandkids that it would take a page to name them all. But you would be proud of each and every one of them. They are all so wonderful.

I remember Vestanna, your oldest granddaughter, missing you a great deal after you died. She told me once when she was very little that she was struggling with the thought of cutting her beautiful long hair. She told me that if she could only go visit with Grandpa, he would help her decide. So, she did. She talked to you as if you were standing right there.

Now your youngest granddaughter, Lindsey, is 20 years old and engaged to be married. It just doesn't seem possible. The grandkids and great grandkids who have come since you passed have only photos and stories to remember you by. But we tell the stories and show the photos so they will know you if only through someone else's memories.

I never had any children of my own, but I had 2 dogs ... Muffin and Lady, my own little fuzzy, four legged kids. I was pregnant once but lost the baby. That was such a sad time in my life and the pain is still as real today as it was almost 21 years ago. Sure would have been nice to have you around to talk to about it.

I participated in the Big Brothers, Big Sisters program and was matched with the most amazing girl for a "Little." Le'Trail and I were "Bigs" and "Littles" for 10 wonderful years. She brought so much joy into my life and many times it seemed like she was more like my own child than a Little in a mentoring program. I'm so very proud of her. She is a young adult now, on her own, attending college and will soon be graduating. My, how time does fly. Sure would have been nice if you could have met her.

We lost Mom almost 13 years ago … well, at least we lost the mom we all knew and depended on. She suffered a terribly debilitating stroke that spring, just two weeks shy of retirement. She lost her ability to walk, to speak, to care for herself, she even lost the ability to move herself from a chair to a bed. Oh, what a time that was. I remember for my 40th birthday we moved Mom into a nursing home. I cried and cried all the way home that day. My sister baked me a birthday cake before Mom's move-in day. Mom was so proud that she was able to frost the cake. Even one-handed and having to tilt her head from side to side just to see it, she still frosted that cake with lightning speed and better than I can even today with two good hands. I still tear up when I have to leave her when I visit. Sure would be nice to have you around to talk to about it.

There isn't a day that goes by that I don't stop and think of you. I had only begun to get to know you when you died. It took many years to get over the feelings of being angry at you. But as all things do, so these feelings passed with time. Sure would have been nice to have you here to help me understand why things were the way they were and maybe even to say … I'm sorry I left.

As a child I looked forward to the times that you would come home to visit. You were like this fun guest that would show up once in a while and would bring a burst of energy into my day. I longed for the days when you would visit. As a teenager I spent many days angry with you that you were not there and it seemed as if you didn't care. As a young adult I looked forward once again to the time that I did get to spend with you. Sure would be nice to have you here now to hear you say … can't wait to spend time with you again.

I remember when you tried to teach me to play the guitar. I bought
a guitar and took it to your apartment and the lessons began. Trying
to sing and play "Down in the Valley" with you was pretty comical.
I still have that guitar and to this day, I still can't play it. In fact it only
has a few strings left on it that are not broken. I still sing a lot, though
— in the shower, in the car with the radio, with the TV, during the
movies, while I'm washing dishes, and when I am feeling sad. I will
sit in the back yard and quietly sing to myself so my neighbors don't
have to suffer. I'm reminded once that during a church service, the
pastor told us, "...now let's all sing that verse again, but this time I
want you all to sing as loud as you can. Sing loud to praise God for
giving you a beautiful voice. Those of you who can't sing well,
I want you to sing even louder just to get even!" I get even ... a lot.
Good or bad, I still like to sing. Sure would be nice now to have you
here to say ... even though you still can't sing, sing anyway. Let's sing
together and let's sing loud.

Time seems to rush by so quickly these days. The older I get the
more my own mortality seems to look me in the face. I never thought
for a minute that I would spend most of my life alone, but that is the
way it has worked out. But I'm not lonely. Maybe I'm more like you
than I realize. Sure would be nice to have you say ... don't worry,
we'll be together again someday and neither one of us will ever be
alone again.

As I close this letter I am reminded of a poem that was scratched
onto a page of one of mom's old autograph books that she had as
a child. *When evening rolls her curtains down, and pins them with a
star, remember that you have a friend, no matter where you are.* You are
remembered, Dad. You are loved. You are forgiven. You are greatly
missed. Sure would be nice to have you here to be able to tell you ...
I love you, Dad.

#7 Kid

FROM: CARLA ASHBY, DAUGHTER

LANEY BOOKER

August 9, 1939~ March 29, 2009

He was the son of Lannie and Victoria Booker, brother of Alvin, Betty, Alma, Madelyn, and Brenda.

He graduated from Booker T. Washington High School, Texarkana, Arkansas, and Cisco Junior College. He served 22 years in the United States Air Force and was a senior master seargent. He then worked for the United States Postal Service until his retirement. He was married to Zonella Faye and was the proud father of Shandra and Stacy and proud grandfather of grandson Jayden. He loved playing golf and being physically fit. He didn't smoke or drink.

Laney died from lung cancer.

Dad,

It seems hard to believe around this time four years ago you started chemo and radiation treatment. Lung cancer happens to other people. Not my dad — who worked out, played golf, watched what he ate, didn't smoke, didn't drink … Cancer shouldn't happen to good people. No one deserves that. Least of all you — I don't think I ever heard you talk bad about someone. You loved Mom and Mom loved you — everyone who knew you saw it. I won't list sacrifices you did for Stacy and I or the pride we all saw when you looked at Jayden.

I hate what cancer did to my family. I hate that Mom is hurting. I hate that if I ever have kids they will never know their Papa.

Jayden — I hurt worse for him. Your grandson loves his baseball. On the anniversary of your passing, Stacy told him to have a good game on you and Nana — and did he ever. Some extra bases, RBIs, the only thing he didn't do was hit a home run. I hope he remembers you. He should have more time with you.

I hope I told you I loved you enough. I hope I told you how proud I am to be your daughter. I do — I am. How many times have I picked up the phone, and have to stop myself for asking for you when I call home. I still catch myself saying I'm going to my parents'. The caller ID on my landline still says "Parents" because I can't bring myself to change it.

I miss our talks. I used to think we wouldn't have anything to talk about after I graduated from college.

Above all, I hope you're still proud of me. I wonder almost every day, when I drive to a job I absolutely hate. Am I wasting the college degrees you paid for? You made so many sacrifices for Stacy and I. I feel like I'm letting you down. I know you probably say I'm not, and that's what fathers are supposed to do.

There is not a day that goes by I don't think of you or miss you. I know I could write more — but I will save that for another letter.

After God called you home, I bought Stacy and I a copy of *Why a Daughter Needs a Dad*. Although there are 100 reasons listed, I always go back to three:

A daughter needs a dad

~ Who will never think she is too old to need him.

~ Who will influence her life even when he isn't with her.

~ So that when no one is there for her, she can close her eyes and see him.

I love you, Dad!

Love, Shandra

FROM: SHANDRA BOOKER, DAUGHTER

GUADALUPE GARCIA

February 22, 1926 ~ March 16, 1994

She was the daughter of Thomas and Guadalupe Carreno, and the sister of Tony, David, Lucian, Joey, Lola, Ruth, Jovita, Helen, and Connie.

She went to Our Lady of Guadalupe School, Topeka, Kansas. She was married to John and they had nine children: Susanna, Carolina, Ramona, Patricia, Rebecca, Edward, James, Barbara, and John, as well as 18 grandchildren and 12 great-grandchildren. She worked at La Siesta Restaurant and many people came just to see her. She loved garage sales and made homemade tortillas for sale.

Lupe died from a viral infection.

Grandma Garcia,

I miss you. You were a social butterfly and I really admired how easily you connected with anyone and everyone. You always had a smile on your face and I can still hear your laugh. You made everyone feel special and loved, including me. I really cherish those memories. I really wish you could have stayed on this earth for a lot longer than you did. You are deeply missed by many people, friends and family alike. This may sound weird, but you had the most beautiful funeral procession that I have ever seen. There must have been 300 cars en route to the cemetery. It brought tears to my eyes because it showed how many people cared and how deeply you would be missed. I really miss your warm, loving arms. And I miss your homemade tortillas! Haha. I was only 19 when you left, but you left such an impression on my heart. I miss you and I love you.

Arminda

FROM: ARMINDA GUERRERO, GRANDDAUGHTER

EDWARD RAY HANKINS

March 19, 1933 ~ July 3, 2000

He was the son of Daniel and Ruth Hankins, and brother of Dee Ann.

He graduated from Winfield High School, Winfield, Kansas, and Pittsburg State Teachers College, Pittsburg, Kansas. He served in the United States Army. He spent his career as a teacher, coach, and administrator.

He was married to Rose Marie (Rosie) and had two children, Ken and Kammi, as well as son-in-law Brad and grandchildren Bryan and Angela. He loved all sports but his passion was tennis. He was a devoted husband, father, and grandfather.

Edward died from a heart attack while playing tennis.

Hi Dad,

It has been several years since we lost you so suddenly. I believe with all my heart you already know the things I am going to share with you. However, Dad, it is important for me ... you know that I KNOW them.

First thank you so dearly for sense of family. Through all things, family gets you there both great and small, happy and sad. As I sit at Mom's writing you this letter I know that you would say there is no better place for me to be while doing this than at her house. Kammi is always there for me, that has never changed a bit either. From taking care of my bullies when I was little, to being there through every little up or down, if I need to talk she always listens.

Second, Dad, is the value of friendship. I don't have your sense of outgoing-ness but I have my good friends who I know I can count on through thick or thin, but most important they add laughter to my days and that seems to be the best medicine a guy could need. I still laugh with many you know — Kim, Maria, Bob, Michael, Larry — and then there are those that I share both the laughter and the tears, such as my dear boys Brad and Bert; and of course Lance. Lance lost both of his parents this year. It was a mixed blessing, of course we all miss them and few more than Lance, but I saw a layer of stress fall off of him in the weeks following. He had devoted much to being their caregiver and I could see it was really wearing him down.

The third thing, Dad, is the value of giving. From you I learned much about giving and the key is giving comes in many forms. Giving of oneself in partnership with another, Eldon and I share a wonderful life together and take great care of each other, just as

you always have known. I also give back to the community by bringing my talents, time, and money to the Mental Health Association.
I started with them by bringing my experience in Information
Technology to their Board of Directors. Today I am in my fifth year
of service with them and bring as Chairman of their Board the
leadership skill from my Ph. D. (Oh, by the way, thanks too for the
appreciation of the value of education, it has given me untold opportunities.) I also give in a very unique way that truly was learned from
you and that is through acceptance in all people. You saw the good
in so many when others may have overlooked it or might have made
no effort to appreciate it. Through your example I try not to be
judgmental but to listen to those who may be different than me
or who may have very different life experiences which shaped the
way they think about the world. Some call this a genuine caring for
people, I don't think you would disagree with that but I think you
would call it basic respect for yourself and of others to do so.

I find many times in my life now I do not have all the answers and
the challenges can overwhelm. It is at these times I so dearly miss
being able to talk to you but I know if you were guiding me you
would tell me to believe in the power of family, to share with friends
and know the power of their healing, and to focus on what I can give,
and not on what I can get or take, and soon life and I will be all the
better for it.

You grateful son, Ken

From: Ken Hankins, son

PHYLLIS MARION HOFFMAN

December 10, 1934 ~ March 2, 2012

She was the daughter of Mike and Mable Wilkinson, and the sister of Duane and Dorothy.

She graduated from Topeka High School, Topeka, Kansas. She worked doing laundry for several nursing homes. She was also a Girl Scout leader for many years. She collected stamps and coins. She had five children, Cindy, Sandy, Brenda, Debbie, and Barbie.

Phyllis died of natural causes.

To my sweet, sweet mother, Phyllis Hoffman

I miss you so much! I miss your smile, your laugh, the way you would pat my cheek when I kissed you goodbye. If I had only known that it was gonna be the last time, I would have stayed longer. I miss you trying to think of just one more thing you needed to tell me before you would let me get out the door. I'm sorry that you were alone for so many years. I miss all the times you would call me and I would answer the phone just in time to hear you say, "Oh damn it! I can't remember what I called you for!" One of the first things I did, was check my phone to see if I still had a message from you in my cell phone. I was so sad to hear that I didn't. I would give anything to hear your voice on the other end of my phone. I have caught myself many times thinking that I needed to call you and tell you something.

Some days I'm mad, because I was the one that found you. Of course I was the one to find you because I was there more than anyone else. And now, that some time has passed, I'm thankful that the odds were stacked against me because that meant that I was privileged to have spent more time with you. I should have set aside more time for you, not just my weekly shopping where I was in and out so quickly. Why is it that we don't realize that until it is too late?

You were always there for me and no matter what else I had going on, if you called and needed me, I was there for you. You knew you could count on me and I'm proud of that!

I know that you knew how much I loved you, but that hasn't made me feel much better yet. I still struggle every day without you here.

I know that you are with many of the people you have missed for many years. You grew up without your mother and now you are with her and your dad. You're with your sister who you have missed so much. I remember going to the nursing home where you worked the day Aunt Dorothy died. You looked at me puzzled and wanted to know what I was doing there. We cried together and held each other. You were such a strong woman. And you're finally with Dad again. I know that you are smiling up there. Your family always meant the world to you.

It's hard to go on without you, and I still can't think about you without crying. I struggle with the picture in my mind of you lying on your bathroom floor the day I found you. I hope that some day I have a better picture up there! Darrell and I talk about you often. About the crush you had on him and how anytime you were around and Darrell was there you would just look at him and do the "Come here" movement with your finger! You always had a special place in your heart for him as he also had for you. I am thankful that we share that love for you, he helps me when I am struggling to go on without you.

I hope that you are as proud to call me your daughter as I am to call you Mom. I love you so much, Mom. I will miss you every single day until we meet again!

Give everyone my love! I love you with all my heart!

Debbie

FROM: DEBBIE VIERGEVER, DAUGHTER

NORMA LEE (GENTRY) McCART

August 28, 1926 ~ October 10, 1969

She was the daughter of Raymond and Alice Gentry, and the sister of Geneva, Bob, Don, Leonard, and Jerry.

She was married to Eugene Denton McCart, who died August 1, 1998. She was the mother of Betty, Bonnie, Denny, Stevie, Terry, Jerry and Alice. She had 19 grandchildren and 25 great-grandchildren.

Her passion was bowling. Besides playing the sport, she worked at the alley and hand embroidered bowling shirts.

She passed away from an aneurysm at age 43.

Mom

Remember when I was eight and I developed a mastoid infection in my right ear? I suffered with it every day until I had surgery when I was nine. As much as it hurt one good thing was I got to spend a lot of time with you during the hour-long drive back and forth to K.U. I remember the first person I saw when I woke up from surgery was you sitting at my bedside. Mom, you were the only one who really seemed to understand the pain that I was going through. I remember you working so hard to help me and encourage me with my passion for art. Even though money was tight you worked hard to supply me everything I could ask for so I could be creative and work at what I hoped I would be one day, an artist.

When you passed away I lost the passion to draw. It just hurt too much to sit down and work with all the wonderful art supplies you bought me. I would sit down and look up at the wall in front of me and see the drawings you hung up that I had done because they were all your favorites. I am sure all of my inspiration came totally from you, every mark or stroke I made with my brush or pencil was made out of the love you gave to me.

Mom, I have not cried over your passing since I was sixteen ... that is, until today while writing this letter. I also haven't felt that love and closeness in my heart since then. I thought that feeling of love that you always gave me was gone forever, but I have to tell you I feel your love today and it is stronger than my pain of losing you.

Mom, I love you and I need to apologize to you for quitting on you when you left me. I tried but it just hurt so much. I would ask for your forgiveness, but I know you have forgiven me. I know because all the warm loving feelings I had from you, I felt them again today. I hope you know that I feel it and am sending my love right back to you.

Terry

FROM: TERRY MCCART, SON

RONALD D. RINEHART

September 21, 1955~ August 30, 1983

He was the son of Glen and Clara Mae Rinehart, and the brother of Sherri.

He graduated from Kendall High School, Kendall, Kansas, and North West Kansas Area Vocational Technical School, Goodland, Kansas. He worked as a pilot for Priority Aviation in Gardner, Kansas. On January 10, 1976, he earned his private pilot's license. He worked for John Deere on diesel engines, and was a professional pilot. He was married to Donna (Kate) Nuessen and they had a daughter, Jennifer, born in 1980. He received his commercial pilot's license in 1980 and his airline transport pilot license in 1983.

Ron was killed in a plane crash.

Dear Dad,

I lost you the day after my third birthday. You have missed so many events in my life that you should have been there for. When I was five years old you missed my first day of school. When I was seven, I had my first communion. There are many more things that you missed during my childhood and teenage years. However the things that I'm most proud of have been since I've graduated high school.

In 2002 we lost Grandma. I knew then what I wanted to do with my life … to take care of people when they are sick, to make a difference in someone's life … I wanted to be a nurse.

In 2004 I married Jack. You weren't there to walk me down the aisle and give me away. That same year Jacob was born and you became a grandpa. I waited for Grandpa Glen to make it to the hospital to have him. Grandpa's eyes lit up when he first saw him.

In 2006 Grandpa died! I learned then more than ever that I wanted to be a nurse. So that spring I graduated L.P.N. school. I started working in a small hospital that fall.

In 2007 Colten was born and you became a grandpa again. My two little boys are the light of my life. We decided to give Colten your middle name "D."

In 2011 I returned to school, graduated, and became an R.N. I love my job and I love helping people when they are sick.

Dad, the thirtieth anniversary is approaching. It's sad to say that I do not remember you; I don't remember the sound of your voice. I do have pictures and Mom and other family members will tell me stories about you. One thing I have noticed is that the older I get the harder it is for me to not have you here with me. I look at my boys now and realize how much you truly have missed. Mom and I are very close and Richard has been there for me since you couldn't be but there are days that I just need my real dad! What I wouldn't give to have you back! I love you, Daddy, and I always will. The boys and I will be watching for your bright shiny star in the sky!

Love, Jenny

FROM: JENNY CLARY, DAUGHTER

HELEN PEARL (MAZE) SCHREINER

May 20, 1929 ~ May 13, 1982

She was the daughter of Archie and Requa Maze, and the sister of Barbara, Bob, Marie, Carrie, Dorothy, and Elizabeth.

She graduated from Topeka High School, Topeka, Kansas, and attended Washburn College. She married Edmund Schreiner and they had five children, Susan, Bruce, Steve, Andy, and Mark, as well as 14 grandchildren and 15 great-grandchildren. She was a homemaker and helped with her husband's concrete business. She enjoyed crafts, singing, animals, reading, and puzzles.

Helen died of bronchial pneumonia.

Mom,

It has been 30 years since I last saw you. I remember leaving for school, my last day of high school. You were lying on the couch, sleeping, where you normally did. Dad had fixed you some toast and coffee. It was on the table beside you. I gave you a kiss, said I loved you and rushed out the door. That was the last time I saw you alive. Who knew that cough that you had was worse than the normal smoker's cough you always had. You had bronchial pneumonia and your lungs filled up.

I never got to have a relationship with you as an adult. I think about you often. You have been an inspiration to me in a lot of ways. You were one of the most giving people I ever met. If someone came to our house and said, "I like that picture." You would say, "Well here, take it, you can have it." Dad used to get so mad at you. When you were in the State Hospital, he would take you a carton of cigarettes and three days later they would be gone. You had made friends and were sharing with them. You kept coming home and tried to get well but never could overcome the depression.

I think of you a lot in the month of May. Mother's Day, Memorial Day and your birthday. I always wondered how you allowed people around you to drive you crazy. I do understand, now, from my own life experiences that even though you marry your best friend, things change. That person can change, break your heart and become your worst enemy. You didn't have the strength to leave. Because of you, I did.

I wish my kids could have known you. I try to keep the traditions started by you, going. I sing "The Teddy Bears Picnic" to them and now to the grandkids. My daughter, Katie, and I make your home-made rolls at least a couple times a year. We also make homemade apple pie, the crust isn't as pretty as yours, but still tastes good. We still have handmade ornaments, that you made, on the Christmas tree every year. Also the ceramic nativity scene. You loved to do crafts, especially ceramics and were able to when you would go to the State Hospital as part of your therapy. I remember when I was little you used to say to me, "If I could change anything about you it would be your hair." It was fine, stick straight and wouldn't hold a curl. My brothers had thick curly hair. Now most of my brothers don't have much hair and I went to beauty school and learned how to do hair. You were also the most honest person I ever met. You wouldn't cheat or steal from anyone. You are my conscience. If I ever start to sway, I can feel you bop in the back of the head and say "Susie, you know better." I tell my kids that Grandma Helen is watching.

I miss you a lot, especially when times are rough and I really wish I had my mom to talk to. I know in my heart that you are there, but it would be nice to have you physically there and be able to give you a hug. Through all the craziness in our house and the abnormalness of it all, I feel very lucky to have had you as my mother. You taught me morals and values that I have tried to pass on to my children. You were too young to die and I wish you could have stayed on this earth a lot longer. You would be very proud of your children, grandchildren and now great-grandchildren. Your granddaughter Gracie and great-granddaughter McKinley both have your middle name, Pearl.

You are gone but not forgotten, forever in our hearts. I love you, Mom.

FROM: SUSAN FLYNN, DAUGHTER

VI

BROTHERS & SISTERS
AND PARTNERS IN LIFE

*There is no love like that between brothers, sisters,
and husbands and wives.*

JONCE JERRUS HUBBLE

December 26, 1968 ~ July 22, 2010

He was the son of Andray Hubble and Connie Patterson, and the brother of Jason, Shane, Joey, and Ashley.

He graduated from Guntersville High School, Guntersville, Alabama. He worked for McCord Communications. He was an Alabama State Wrestling Champion. He served in the United States Marine Corps. He loved riding motorcycles, raising money for St Jude's Research Hospital, spending time at the lake, and spending time with family and friends. He was married to Bridgette, and was the father of Matthew, Jonce, Dray, and Destiny. For more information visit the Hubble Foundation.

Jonce died in a fall from a tower he was working on.

Dearest Hunny Bunn,

I miss you. I love you. I have been able to feel you every day since
you left. A simple breeze, the flutter of a butterfly, certain sounds,
smells, and sensations often trigger your face and laugh to my mind.
I have had every range of emotion, temper tantrum, and hissy fit
since that day. I have literally felt every single emotion simultaneously.
You were taken from me far too soon and far too tragically. I never in
my wildest dreams pictured living my life without you in it, and there
is not a day that goes by that I don't think of you, miss you, or love
you. So much has happened in the past two years. Some days it feels
like you were just taken from me, other days it feels as though it has
been so much longer than two years.

When you died, I was left with a huge void I never thought would be
filled. God watched me, felt my pain, and, in my private moments,
He let me rage with anger and irreconcilable loss. Soon after, though,
He calmed that rage & sadness, replaced it with Peace, and *He
reconciled me.* You have left this world, but you didn't leave me. Your
heart, your love, and our memories are with me always and even
though you are not here with me, you live through me. *You were a part
of who I was, who I am.*

You have returned to see me, and I know you are happy, safe, and
blissful with God … we've had that conversation. You know the path
my life has taken, that I have remarried, that I am almost done with
school, and that I fight (or try to) to champion your memory and the
others that climb. I know that you are near me, and I know you have
looked over me since you went home. You know that I carry on, push
forward, try to honor your memory, and that I am happy once again
… we have had that conversation, too.:)

I will always remember your death, but I *cherish and celebrate* your life
and the memories we made together. I am not sad anymore, I am not
bitter; God filled that void with peace. God has a plan, and although

I don't know what that is, I will eventually. Knowing you are there with Him, and that you are safe, whole, and happy is enough for me until we are able to be together again.

All of my Love,

-Me- <3

P.S. Hunny Bunn. B-E-H-A-V-E ….and don't annoy Bear Bryant … I want him in a good mood when I get there :) Love you, baby….

FROM: BRIDGETTE HUBBLE, WIFE

JULIE ANN LUMAN

February 23, 1961 ~ August 17, 1979

She was the daughter of Buddy and Marie Luman, and the sister of Lisa, Bruce, and Amy.

She graduated from Rossville High School, Rossville, Kansas, and was attending Clark School of Business, Topeka, Kansas. She loved gardening, horses, and crafts.

Julie died in an auto accident.

Dear Julie,

The memory and reality of your death is forever a part of me as if I am reliving it in the moment. I love you and miss you more than any human being can imagine unless they've lost a sibling themselves. I've always said it cannot be described, only experienced. I miss you. I wanted to tell you what happened after you and Bruce were in the accident … after you were taken from me.

Finally, there was a knock on the door. "Julie's dead." Our father's words seemed distant. Like I was dreaming. I looked around and saw friends I have known for my entire life. They hold tissues, wipe tears, cry quietly. I think to myself, "I should be crying." So I try. I can't. I am numb. I don't remember the ride back to our house. As I sit in the living room, staring at your picture, praying to it as though it would make you come back, our mother makes phone calls. Everyone she talks to hears the words … "Julie's gone … she didn't make it." I hear those words over and over as she tells relatives, friends.

Gone … that word. I don't realize what it means exactly. My mother explains a few things to me. "You are the oldest child now, and you will have more responsibilities. You will need to grow up now." Julie, what does she mean I'm the oldest child now? I'm only 11 years old. What about our brother? I thought he was alive, in the hospital. Maybe he was dead and they just didn't tell me yet. I don't ask.

I am in the way in the kitchen. The grownups are in there talking, crying, weeping … I ask again for something in case I puke. Mom and Dad scream at me. "GET OUT OF HERE!" I run out of the kitchen. I finally start to cry. My mother follows me into the living room. Her finger points very close to my face and she hisses quietly … "YOU STOP YOUR CRYING RIGHT NOW! YOU ARE GOING TO SCARE YOUR LITTLE SISTER! DO YOU UNDERSTAND ME? STRAIGHTEN UP RIGHT NOW!!" I stop crying. I glance up at your picture and I still feel sick. I just wanted you to come back. So desperately. I'm so scared.

I go downstairs to get out of the way. One of our parents' friends is folding laundry for our mother. She looks at me. I remember saying,

"Now Julie can't go to college and become a secretary." She doesn't respond. She stares, and I wonder if I said something I shouldn't have, so I stop talking to her.

I am in the back of the station wagon on the way to the hospital. The car comes to a stop. I spring up to look out the back window. I surprise the people in the car behind us. They don't know who I am. But, they smile and wave at me. I wave back. I don't smile. I think about how they don't know what has happened today. I think about how if they knew, they wouldn't wave at me. They would leave me alone. Like everyone was doing. We drive away ... but I stare at those people ... my hands against the window. Wishing they knew that I felt sick.

We are at the hospital now. There are so many people there. Friends from your high school, friends of our parents. Everyone starts hugging and crying. I didn't cry. I couldn't cry. Amy and I leave with Kenny and ride to his house in the yellow VW Beetle. We get to the house and Barbara leads us to her daughters' room. There, she wakes Donna and Allyson and asks them to move to pallets on the floor so that Amy and I can sleep in their beds. Donna gets up and gives me a hug. She is only seven years old. She makes me feel the safest so far.

I lie in Donna's bed. Barbara says I can listen to the radio. "Someone's knockin' at the door ... somebody's ringin' the bell ... someone's knockin' at the door ... somebody's ringin' the bell ... do me a favor ... open the door ... and let 'em in." Was this a sign? Heaven letting me know that you had knocked at their door and someone needed to let you in? Next, your favorite piano song came on ... "Music Box Dancer." How odd ... remember you had gone out and bought that piano music for me? I learned it as soon as you brought it home. You said, "Lisa, you can play this for me, right? I LOVE this song!! It is so pretty ... will you learn it for me?" Your friends would ask me to play it when they came over. Your friends liked me. You liked me. I wondered if I'd play that song again. I can't remember if I cried myself to sleep. I think I'd remember that.

The next few days are a blur. I try to be good as best I can. One morning I am sleeping on the couch and I wake up just as our mother is leaving to go back to the hospital. I quickly sit up and say,

"Mama!" … but my mother keeps going. She wasn't even out the door yet. How could she not hear me? I lay back down and my feelings are hurt. A lump in my throat burns. I don't cry, though. I'm not supposed to.

One day I am playing a game in the basement with Barbara and Kenny's kids. Barbara brings a grocery bag down and asks me to put it in the laundry room. I notice a small spot of something on the bag. I wonder if it is blood. I wonder if it is your clothes. I open the bag. There are your cut-offs … frayed and worn. And covered in blood. There is your blue summer shirt, the one that ties behind your back … the one I watched you tie in the bathroom the day you left … the last day I saw you. When I run outside to tell you I love you, you turn and say, "I Love You" … and the hot August wind wisps through your hair … and as you turn your back the tie of your blue shirt is also blowing in the wind. And I think … "I love you," and I go inside to play "Music Box Dancer." Now my precious memories of your clothes are tainted by the saturation of colors … brown, black, red … old and dried blood. My last memory of seeing you alive is ruined. I drop the bag and go to Barbara's piano, and I play "Music Box Dancer."

Our grandparents take Amy and me to the funeral home where you are in a room in a casket. I have never seen one before. It is closed. How come I can't see you? I am eyeing the handles on the sides of the casket and wonder if I were to grab one and lift up, would you really be in there? I think about all the things I have heard my parents tell other people. "We never even identified her … she was all cut up … they said we shouldn't see her … she was in too bad of shape." Nobody saw you? I swallow hard and ask, "is she in there?" "Yes, she is in there, honey." My grandfather. I want to ask him if he saw you, but I don't. I'm still scared.

Your funeral. Suddenly I am in Rossville again. I'm not at Barbara's. I didn't realize that I felt so safe there. We pull into the parking lot of the high school. Nobody talked to me, or told me anything. What are we doing here? I look around as I walk. I see relatives and friends. I walk through the long, narrow hallway of concrete. Above me, to my left and right, and below me … all concrete. I start to feel like I can't breathe. The end of the hallway is here, I look in and there is a casket in the middle of the gym surrounded with flowers. On either side of the casket, flowers on the top, flowers all around … flowers on the floor around the casket ... and one picture. The picture of you. The picture I prayed to on the night you died. And suddenly I realize ... you're dead.

I start to panic. I start to cry. I start to scream inside myself. I am flying into a million pieces. "Julie! Come back! Where are you? I have your clothes! I want to play 'Music Box Dancer' for you! JUST PLEASE, PLEASE COME BACK! You said, 'I love you' when you left!" My thoughts were screaming in my head. I am sobbing and cannot get my breath. Nobody notices me, I am scared. And though the gym is full, I am alone.

I kept pleading in my mind, "Please ... come back. How come you are leaving me now? You don't really want to leave me, do you? What did I do? All I did was run out to say 'I Love You,' and you turned to tell me that you loved me, too. I should have said, 'see you later,' I'm sorry ... I'M SORRY!!! Please, I'll give ANYTHING if you will come back to me. Nobody loves me like you do. Nobody."

Sobbing, holding my tummy, staring at your casket ... your picture. That beautiful picture of you with your pretty hair and your cheek resting on your hands ... soft and kind eyes ... I try to focus on your eyes in that picture. I try to feel safe by looking at them. They are still very kind. But, they do not move.

How do I live now? Who will help me with my homework? Who am I going to kiss goodnight now? Every night you expect that I will approach you with a kiss goodnight. You welcome it. You love me. I'll never get that feeling back. Not from anyone. PLEASE ... come back. I can't live without you. You make me feel so safe, so loved ... so understood. Your smile, and your eyes ... they make me feel better ... but your eyes still do not move. You are gone. You died. Your eyes will not move again. Soft and kind, loving and gentle. I'll never lose the memory of your eyes, and the feeling I got from them. Or hearing your voice call out in the hot, summer's wind ... "I LOVE YOU."

Thank you for loving me ... forever, Lisa

FROM: LISA CONAWAY, SISTER

JAMES MICHAEL "COWBOY" SIMS

March 23, 1951 ~ June 1, 2011

He was the son of Willard and Helen Sims, and brother of Loyd, Tom, Barbara, and Beverly.

He graduated from Augusta High School, Augusta, Kansas, and worked for Cessna Aircraft for 36 years. He had many interests and was devoted to his wife, Cindy, and their sons, Shane, Matt, and Bill (who preceded him in death). Jim had many friends but none closer than best friend, Jim Landrum.

Jim died of a brain tumor.

To Jim — Cowboy — Sims

Jimmy, I always felt we would share the benefit of retirement together.
I had envisioned many drinks by the campfire at the cabin, days and
nights at the lake with motorhomes, I guess it wasn't meant to be.
Jim, I left Cessna in 1976, but I never lost contact with you. Even
when I moved for 15 years to KC, whenever I saw that 25-mile sign
to Wichita, I called you. The majority of the time you answered
and I stopped by, sometimes spending the night. How does that
happen? Well sometime between our first meeting — me, the old
crusty beyond his years rebellious Vietnam Vet, and you, this young
man whose wife was with your first child, a country boy who I
dubbed as "Cowboy" — well, we became inseparable. I was there
when you lost your son. I cried with you. You and your parents were
there when I lost Mom and Dad. No one could guide me better than
you. You watched me negotiate good jobs and make good money,
and when the bad times came you tried to encourage me out of it,
but just like when you lost your son, I was not going to be encouraged above it. I was sixty years old when an opportunity came, a dol-
lar short and a day late, but I negotiated and you were amazed at my
demands, but you also knew the hardships of last two years, they did
not. I went for broke on what I knew I could produce and the value
of it, and won. Then I performed and when I called you as I pro-
gressed, unlike other people, you knew me, and you would caution
me to not blow it, be political and keep my cool. I did, all because
of your words of encouragement, you see nobody knew me like you,
Jim, nobody. I wanted to enjoy retirement with your companionship,
and now you are gone. I am brokenhearted! I hate it! I miss you!

Big Jim

FROM: JIM LANDRUM, FRIEND

135

BARRY MARSHALL SLOAN

October 6, 1972 ~ July 22, 2010

He was the son of Terry and Debbie Sloan, and the brother of Andy and Nathan.

He attended Hatley High school, Hatley, Alabama. He worked for McCord Communications. He loved wakeboarding, dirt bikes, fishing and dirt track racing. He loved God. He was married to Ali and was the father of Brooklyn Jade, Breanna, Callie Beth, and Jakob. He loved his family.

Barry died in a fall from a cell tower he was working on.

Barry,

First of all I would like to say I love you and miss you very much.
Sometimes it just doesn't seem fair that you are no longer with us.
Barry, you completed me. You were my best friend and my soul mate.
As we all know my world revolved around you. Since the day you
went to be with our father in heaven I feel as though a part of me
died with you. I struggle with the pain daily and pray that one day
God will heal my broken heart. I came to Lake Guntersville to write
you this letter because I know how much you loved the water. Sometimes I take things like this for granted but then I am reminded of
how selfish it is. I am thankful to have had the opportunity to write
you although it doesn't feel the same. I wish I could see your smile
and give you the biggest hug ever. Above all else I want you to know
how blessed I am to have ever met you. Our story seems like something you only see on movies. I guess this was my fairy tale because
without a doubt I know I met my Prince Charming. You had my
heart @ hello and I will never forget that day. Thank you, Barry, for
loving me and being the best husband ever. There is no one in this
world who can erase the memories we shared because they are close
to my heart. The time I spent with you was the best years of my life.
I can't thank God enough for you. Well, baby, I must go but until we
meet again know that you are loved and missed dearly.

Love Always,

Alison Sloan

FROM ALISON SLOAN, WIFE

DANIEL FRANCIS TEBBETTS

January 24, 1953 ~ May 15, 2009

He was the son of Ralph and Olive Tebbetts, and brother of Ralph, Alan, Patricia, Donna, and Mary.

He graduated from Wantagh High School, Wantagh, Long Island, New York. He was a Vietnam veteran in the United States Army. He was married to Jennell and the father of April and Neil, he was devoted to his family. He was a longtime business owner in Emporia, Kansas. His passion was cars; he loved to race and restore them.

Dan died from bladder cancer.

Dan,

I love you and miss you each and every day of my life. I don't understand why you had to go, but I will not question the will of our Lord. He knows all and I know so little. Who am I kidding? I know nothing. My heart is so broken, I sometimes think that it will never heal. There are days when I feel some healing and days when I feel none at all. You loved me so much and so un-conditionally. I knew how much you loved me, you never failed to tell me and you showed me in all you did to make our life together good. I didn't always let you know it, but I knew just how much you loved me. Our life together was so more than I ever imagined it could be. Thank you!!!!!!!!!!!! Our life was not perfect, but you were perfect for me. I don't think anyone else on this planet could ever deal with your crazy J (hard to love, hard to love). You did it well and with such devotion. You kept my crazy feet on the ground, you were my strength!!! Remember that song I sang to you so often, "Because you loved me "? I always cried, because the lyrics in the song said it all. I am truly everything I am, because you loved me !!!!

Love,

J

FROM: JENNELL TEBBETTS, WIFE

THE SONGS

MUSIC AS THERAPY

M ANY NARRATIVE THERAPISTS are now using music and songs in their work with individuals, groups, and communities. Hospitals, hospices, nursing and assisted-living facilities increasingly employ the services of Certified Music Practioners to provide comfort, assist in transitioning, and aid in healing. This book includes 16 songs based on letters printed on the preceding pages.

The songs are meant to complement the written word. While there is much healing available in writing, the written word is not always accessible to everyone. Songs and music can include most people, and can touch and soothe the soul in a way that the written word often cannot. Please be encouraged to listen to the recording as you read this book, the lyrics are included so sing along if you choose.

Working with producer/engineer Jim Barnes at the Art House in Lawrence, Kansas, and in concert with the letter writers, I have attempted to write music and add words that bring the letters to life musically.

The following musicians contributed to this project:

JIM BARNES: Drums, background vocals, keyboards, as well as production, engineering and arrangement assistance

TERRY McCART: Piano ("Too High a Price to Pay")

JOHN FLYNN: Lead Guitar ("Too High a Price to Pay") as well as the use of his home studio for additional recording.

ARMINDA GUERRERO: Flute ("Tommy," "Of Course")

ZACHARY PEREZ: Cello ("Tommy," "Janie")

HERSCHEL STROUD: Trumpet ("Tommy")

VON KOPFMAN: Guitar, bass, lead guitar, lead vocals, background vocals, production, arrangements (all songs)

SONGS *for* HEALING

To access the songs, click on this QR code:

NEVER SAY GOODBYE

WORDS: VON & JORDAN KOPFMAN
MUSIC: VON KOPFMAN

I wonder what you were thinking, as you fell from the sky
Did everyone you'd loved before, pass there before your eyes
I hope the last thing you ever saw, was the perfect sky so blue
I hope your very last thought, was how much I love you

I know you're someplace magical, some call paradise
Free from imperfection, in every way all right
And I know someday I'll join you, and I'll look into your eyes
Each day until that moment, let's never say goodbye

They say you did not suffer, and you felt no pain
In an instant it was over, and you just slipped away
I hope when you got where you were going, nothing could compare
You're surrounded by those who've gone before and you're waiting for me there

TRUE COWBOY

WORDS: RENÉE HIVELY, SETH HIVELY, VON KOPFMAN
MUSIC: VON KOPFMAN

Everywhere I go there is something that reminds me of you
And I try to choke back the tears, that's what a cowboy's supposed to do
If you get a chance after you ride across that big old sky tonight
Would you ask God to send a sign to let us know that you're all right

You lived your dream, you were a true cowboy
You were our everything, you brought us so much joy
You may have ridden off into the sunset, and be dancing with the stars
But you will never ride out of our hearts

The wind is blowing, still no rain, your memories heavy on my mind
And it's driving me insane, so much pain; I wish I had a little more time
I try not to show any weakness, but my heart hurts so bad today
I guess I need to cowboy up; yeah I'm sure that's what you'd say

I keep telling myself you're out on some roping adventure
And soon I'll see you, on your horse trotting across the pasture
You'll burst into the back door, wearing that great big smile
I know it's not real, at least I can dream for a while

It's been three months and this hole in my heart won't heal
I love and miss you every second, I'm more empty than I ever thought I'd feel
The next chapter of our lives has nearly been erased
Your little brother's the only thing that can still put a smile on our face

FIVE MORE MINUTES

WORDS: JORDAN KOPFMAN, VON KOPFMAN
MUSIC: VON KOPFMAN

You can't leave me now you're the most important thing to me
Who will be there in my time of need
I hit the punching bag but the rage won't be contained
I drink to numb the pain, the emotions they stay the same

I'm tired of crying, I feel like I'm dying inside
I just wanted five more minutes of you in my life
I ask my higher power how HE could take you from me
Jacob I love you please let me know you're at peace

Who will be my best man and give me advice
Who'll be the favorite uncle and walk by my side
You're there making friends as always while I'm here with a broken heart
Someday I'll join you and we'll never be apart

I'm tired of crying I feel like I'm dying inside
I just wanted five more minutes with you in my life
I'll never forget you as the years go by
I just wanted five more minutes to tell you goodbye

You can't leave me now, you're the most important thing to me

ONE MORE ANYTHING

WORDS: BILL MANWARING, JACKIE MANWARING,
VON KOPFMAN
MUSIC: VON KOPFMAN

Where can I start, how can I express all I feel
You had such a way of touching a heart that was real
The love that you gave, the respect shown for family
You openly offered love to your brother and me

Give me one more hello, one more hug, one more smile
One more I love you, one more fishing trip, one more mile
I need one more conversation, one more memory, and one more song to sing
All I can ask is please just, one more anything

The dimples when you smile, your big beautiful blue eyes
The way you said hello, I wish I could have told you goodbye
Though you faced some battles I always knew you would win
I pray you're at peace and I'm sure I will see you again

I wish things could have been different
in those years when you needed me most
So much that happened
Was beyond our control

BLUE WINGS

WORDS: KAREN KOPFMAN, RAY KOPFMAN, VON KOPFMAN
MUSIC: VON KOPFMAN

Our worst fears confirmed, when we heard you were gone
Our hearts are broken; we'll never be the same
For personal reasons, I never believed in a God
Now I'm begging him to let me take your place

I always believed in angels, now you're one watching over me
Would you ask God if you can have blue wings, so you're easy to see

You probably thought we were silly
To worry about you so, it's a grandparent's prerogative
It is so hard to let you go
I'm convinced that I'll see you again

We are hurting because we lost you
We should rejoice because you were here

Do you know how much we miss you and your really sweet smile,
You're my guardian angel from now on

JANIE

WORDS: MARILYN SCHROEDER, VON KOPFMAN
MUSIC: VON KOPFMAN

Hello, Mom, so nice to see you today, I wish it were anywhere but here
I close my eyes and everything's OK; I have my faith so I have nothing to fear
Remember when we'd go to the antique store, or out to eat,
　　　oh we had good times
Mom, I'm so proud of all we shared, it makes me smile when those thoughts
　　　come to mind

What should I tell Tommy?
I know I'm gonna see him soon
Though I hate leaving
God's got something for me to do
Should I tell him that you love him
And how you miss him I suppose
What should I tell Tommy
I'll bet he already knows

When you're sad, think of Cherokee, I'm riding
Mane and tail are flying

You know I'm so tired, Mom, I think it's time to let go
I believe, I believe there is healing where the streets are paved with gold
And I'll be as close as the next remember when, before you know
　　　we'll be together again

OF COURSE

WORDS: AMY MCLAREN, VON KOPFMAN
MUSIC: VON KOPFMAN

Holding hands in the car, no words need spoken
It was fun watching you grow to hold other girls' hands
I knew you would have been an excellent husband
But, Andy, you never got the chance

I'm here looking over the ocean, created by God's mighty hand
I'm sure everything that happens is part of the Master's plan
Two things I am sure of, our reunion will be so so sweet
And this part of the plan revealed, now the circle is complete
The reasons straight from the Source, whose will must be enforced
The veil lifted, the purpose endorsed, Of Course, Of Course

You seemed to grow so tall in that last year
Your presence so huge, I can still feel you here
You'd come in to talk or just to hang out
You never seemed embarrassed by us, there's no doubt

You will forever be sixteen in my memory
I pray those memories stay clear
I fear they might fade away; the sound of your voice slowly fades
The warmth of your touch, even now the thought brings me to tears

TOMMY

WORDS: MARILYN SCHROEDER, VON KOPFMAN
MUSIC: VON KOPFMAN

So many great memories, your quick wit your emotional strength
You were always there for your dad and me, willing to do whatever
      we would need
You would be so happy to see how Erica is flowering; she's a beautiful
      ten-year-old
So much like you, her mother told me so, Oh, Tom, you are always on my mind

Marci's a fabulous mother I'm sure you know, she's provided a stable
      and loving home
So much has changed in the past ten years, your sister Janie is no longer here
The reunion the two of you must have shared

I loved your intelligence and your sense of humor
The day you were born was my happiest day, so well-mannered
      so well behaved
Oh, Tom, such good memories you left behind

You worked so hard every day, going to school you paid your own way
That you held your daughter I'm so glad, I know you'd have been
      a wonderful dad
And I know your presence is always near

You were so proud playing your trumpet in the K.U. marching band
So proud to be a Jayhawk right up until the end

I don't know what to believe of the afterlife, But I hope that this isn't
      all that there is
Maybe Janie's belief was right and you're together with your big sis
Tom, you made a big impact in your short time

No Right to Leave

WORDS: JEAN POWELL, VON KOPFMAN
MUSIC: VON KOPFMAN

I don't know how to live like this, my mind can't comprehend
Not one more hug not one last kiss, never touching you again, never again
I am so scared my memories will fade, the sound of your voice,
slipping away
Trying to analyze the last words you said, like a movie playing over
in my head

I don't want to be this person; I don't want to feel this pain
I cry and cry all the time; I don't want to feel this way
What did I do for you to feel, you couldn't confide in me
What made you think you had the right to leave

I'll never know exactly why, I suppose, People say words cause they don't
know what to do
They tell me you're my guardian angel you know, I don't need an angel,
Steven, I need you

Your dad needs his son; your siblings need their brother
But you took that all away
And I'm trying to pick up the pieces
And pretend that I'm OK, but I'm not OK

I pray you've found peace and happiness, that's all I ever wanted for you
Just wish that could have happened with us, Please know I will always
love you, Steven, I love you

MAGICAL THINKING

WORDS: JOAN DIDION, VON KOPFMAN
MUSIC: VON KOPFMAN

I'm waiting for that familiar hello,
I'm expecting any minute you will be home
Your shoes right where you left them on the floor
Your robe on the hook just inside the bathroom door
I hope it's not my mind playing tricks on me
You've been gone so long, it just might be magical thinking

Your book where you left it on the chair
The firewood where you stacked it on the hearth over there
The papers you bought with intentions to read
Your favorite sweater with the stains on the sleeve
Could it be my mind is playing tricks on me
You've been away so long, but it can't be magical thinking

I was there making dinner when you disappeared
I heard what the doctor was saying but it wasn't too clear
Your things are as you left them right here
And any day now I am sure you will reappear.

And what about our daughter she still doesn't know
Every day I go to the hospital all alone
And though I know the finality to it all
Every time the phone rings I assume it's your call
I guess my mind is playing tricks on me
You've been gone so long, it has to be magical thinking

TAKE ME

WORDS: STAN ALLDREDGE, VON KOPFMAN
MUSIC: VON KOPFMAN

It's been ten years since you were taken away from us
I long to talk to you once again
There's not a day that goes by you aren't on my mind
I miss my son I miss my best friend
When you slipped from our lives,
So many things you know they changed

I pray there's an afterlife, you're in a better space
There's still a hole in my heart where you used to be
And I'd sell my soul if I could take your place
Every day I beg God to leave you, and take me

Your friends keep in touch with me and your brother
Your memory has not been forsaken
I watch them progress it makes me wonder
What you would have become and why you were taken
I'm grateful we got to come and see you, the week before the accident
took you away

Please watch over Andy you know he needs you so I pray every day
for his peace of mind
It's been so hard for me to let you go and for all you left behind

Your mother and I grew apart after your passing,
please know we both love and miss you so much

TAKE MY BREATH

WORDS: LORI BURKE, VON KOPFMAN
MUSIC: VON KOPFMAN

I want to tell you I'm sorry for the things I didn't do right
I didn't want you to go I didn't know why
You said I could come, and that you'd be fine
I trusted God, you kissed my cheek and walked out of my life

Now your voice and laughter are gone, and silence fills the air
I begged God to take my breath, so you could still be here

I want to tell you how much a joy you were to me
Hey watch this, Momma; you always had something for me to see
My love for you was always stronger than my fear
If I couldn't have saved you, I'd have died trying, that's clear

I miss your hugs and kisses; I miss your words of love
I miss the light in your big blue eyes; I miss you my son

I want to tell you I'm grateful for your spirit visiting
At least I know that in spite of my failings you still love me
I love you more than life and all it can bring
And I was blessed to be your mom, oh Ben, you meant everything

PENNIES

WORDS: BRENDA FUTRELL, VON KOPFMAN
MUSIC: VON KOPFMAN

It's been a long time five years since you passed
Didn't know how I'd survive, oh, I just want you back
You were an unexpected blessing such an unimagined loss
Though we couldn't say goodbye I know you're near, 'cause I keep coming across

Pennies from heaven
Every time I look down that's what I see
Are you trying to send out a message
'Cause I swear I saw Abraham winking at me

I feel your presence, sometimes it's just a little sign
A coin on the sidewalk, all the photos you left behind
By now you're with your dad, I guess I'm glad he's there with you
Losing you both hurts so bad, still your signal keeps coming through

Pennies from heaven
Like a little piece of your heart for all to see
And I feel you're communicating
'Cause I know I saw Abraham winking at me

Life has gone on but it's just not the same
But every time I find a penny it puts a smile on my face

FULL THROTTLE

WORDS: TOM AUGUSTYN, VON KOPFMAN
MUSIC: VON KOPFMAN

Where do I begin, you loved the wind in your face
There you'd go again off to the next place
To work or to play, you always seemed to move so fast
You didn't have to be first, you weren't about to be passed
You didn't want to be last

You were never a disappointment, just a heartache sometimes
The second son of a second son, you were loved in this life
You rode this ride your own way, you cut your own path
No time to take a break, full throttle never half

I miss you so much I miss your laughter and your tears
You're in every breath I take you're in all my hopes and fears
You're forever nineteen, you lived so much in your short time
There wasn't much in life you missed, not many things you didn't try
It's so hard to say goodbye

As I travel down this trail, this road called life
I can feel your spirit with me, I'll see you on the other side

TOO HIGH A PRICE TO PAY

WORDS AND MUSIC: VON KOPFMAN

No one knows the hell I'm going through, since you have gone away
Each day I put a smile on like some well-worn shirt, so that no one
sees my pain

But inside a part of me has died, and I'm dying more and more each day
When I'm alone, tears for you fill my eyes, losing you was too high a
price to pay

People say how I seem so strong; they can't believe that I'm so well
What they can't know is I'm not the same; I bury the brokenness so they
can't tell

But inside my heart wants to explode, nothing seems to take the hurt away
When I'm alone the emotions uncontrolled, losing you was too high a
price to pay

Only God has the answers, why things turned out this way

Still I wake up every morning, I greet you hoping that you'll hear
Going through the motions counting down the days, death no longer holds
any fear

But inside I just want to scream, it's never going to be OK
When I'm alone I come apart at the seams, losing you was too high a
price to pay
Losing you was too high a price to pay

JULIE

WORDS AND MUSIC: VON KOPFMAN

She was like a sister and i know how much you miss her
and I know you can still feel that sting

I believe that she is near whispering in your ear just be still
she's still in everything

Julie's in the fresh flowers that dance before your eyes
Julie's in your favorite songs and all those butterflies
Julie's in the photographs and right here in this room
Julie's in your every thought and everything you do

She was your confidandt and the keeper of your secrets
and I know you just needed more time

And I am certain that she knows how you love and need her so
but you can still hear her if you try

Julie's in the sunshine and every drop of rain
Julie's riding shotgun when you're on the road again
Julie's in the summer breaze that messes up your hair
Julie's in your closet telling you what not to wear

We want to live forever and I believe we do
Julie will always be there inside of you

Julie's in Colorado headed down the slopes for fun
Julie's in Arizona trying to keep out of the sun
Julie's in California standing on the shore
Julie's in Houston, Texas, laughing with you once more.

"The word that is heard perishes,
but the letter that is written remains."

– PROVERBS

"Music is what feelings sound like."

– GEORGE CATES

Afterword

NINE YEARS AGO Von was moved to put pen to paper with the publication of the first edition of *Letters for Healing*. Since then, it has inspired, moved, and touched many a person. With this updated edition, it is my hope that the timeless themes will speak to those needing to hear the message that love and connection trumps loss no matter how deep. My words penned then still ring true: I would remind the reader that this project, *Letters for Healing*, was born out of tragedy—the loss of the author's son Jacob. Jacob's death wrought indescribable heartache and pain of an intensity and depth one can only imagine. I have been honored to have been part of Von's healing process around that loss.

When Von, and his surviving son, each discovered that writing letters enhanced their recovery efforts, Von suspected that others could also find comfort in such an outlet. And as simply as that, an idea was born. Not the idea per se of writing for healing, as those who lose loved ones often turn to journaling and letter writing as an emotional outlet in the grieving process. No, Von's idea was to gather together such deeply personal letters of remembrance to stir hope and encouragement for others who are struggling with their losses.

My hope for the reader, now as before, is that you have been touched and inspired by the breadth and depth of feeling in the letters you have read herein, and in the accompanying music. May your perspectives on life and the love you have shared with others experience a renewed healing.

DR. JONATHAN M. FARRELL-HIGGINS

Jonathan M. Farrell-Higgins has been in private practice for more than 30 years, all of it in association with Shadow Wood Clinical Associates. He received his bachelor's degree in psychology from the University of Illinois at Urbana-Champaign and his master's degree and Ph.D in clinical psychology from the University of Kansas. Dr. Farrell-Higgins completed his psychology internship at the Topeka Veteran's Administration Medical Center in 1988.

WRITE YOUR OWN LETTER

WHEN YOU ARE FACED WITH THE LOSS of a loved one or close friend, you will often experience feelings of anger, anxiety or depression. Writing your thoughts down on paper where you can see them, either in a letter to yourself or to the lost loved one, is an effective way to deal with those feelings and begin your journey toward healing.

Often, the hardest thing about writing a letter is the beginning. How do you start?

One method to begin is to try writing ten to fifteen minutes each day. And don't get caught up in thinking, "I'm not a writer" or "I don't know the proper rules of letter writing." It is not necessary to have been an English major or to adhere to the rules of proper English usage. Write from the heart, as if the lost loved one is right there in front of you.

Emily Post writes in *Etiquette:* "Never think, because you cannot write a letter easily, that it is better to not write at all. The most awkward note imaginable is better than none at all."

Write in your own voice, in a conversational style. Write whatever random thoughts you have regarding the loss, or whatever random things you would say to the lost loved one if you had the opportunity to do so.

One method to help organize your thoughts is to keep a journal or conversation diary, where you log your emotions as you feel them. It might help to ask yourself any of these questions:

~ What happened? What do I feel? How am I behaving?

~ How will this affect my day-to-day life? What adjustments will I need to make as it results to everyone and everything else?

~ What can I control today? Can I change this situation? (Then work toward controlling what you can control, and stop trying to control what you cannot.)

~ Who can help me with this problem?

~ Do I need to seek professional help?

~ What can I do to allow myself to begin to relax?

~ What can I be grateful for? Could it have been worse?

~ What, if anything, was left unsaid? Were there unresolved issues
  to address before the healing can begin?

The letter you write may be short or long. You might need to write only once. Perhaps an ongoing series of letters feels right to you. Whatever the case, I encourage you to do it and begin your journey toward healing.

The pages that follow are for you to write your own letter. Remember, there are no rules, there is no right way to do this. It is simply the doing that is important.

Von Kopfman

ACKNOWLEDGMENTS

THIS BOOK AND THESE SONGS are the result of the labor of many hands. And I would like to thank the following for their time, talents, expertise and dedication to this project.

First, on a personal level, I want to thank GOD, my surviving children, my son Jordan and my daughter Kierston along with her husband Charlie and daughter Brynn, my parents Ray and Karen Kopfman, my sister and her family Sara, Dan, Cade and Sadie Pearson, all my extended family, Peg Witmer, The Blue Dot family, Jancy Pettit, Steve Bough, Blake Heath, Walt McFarland, Marti Hill, Hayden Kirby, Rhiannon Foust, Russ Foust, Clyne and Jayce Foust, Mackenzie Hill, Patricia Nichols, Stephen Kirby, Brian and Robin Brown, Mike Gormley, Scott and Karolyn Morgan, Jackie Theis, Jim Gore, Eric Mardis, Eric Keating, Alex Ganger, Scott Grotbeck, Twila Theimer, Jill Foster, J.T.Z., Ray Ortega, Rosie Hankins, Craig Garber, Cali Rider and family, Faith Lutheran Church Topeka Kansas, Bob Shively, Dr. Roy Jensen and Bill Ligon.

Next for their contributions to the book and songs, I want to thank Jim Barnes, Arminda Guerrero, Doug Weaver, Gary Marx, D.J. Matheny, Tara Dimick, Dan and Lisa Mauer and Klik Kreative, Greg Louganis, Lynn Jenkins Katzfey, Jeffrey Gitomer, Dr. Jon Farrell-Higgins, Zach Perez, Herschel Stroud, Otto D'Ambrosio at Eastman Guitars and Ted Kornblum at Magnatone Amps.

To all of the families who trusted me with their letters, their stories, and their lost loved ones, thank you.

A part of the proceeds from this book goes toward the Jacob Von Kopfman Scholarships through Burlington High School, Burlington, Kansas, which promote attendance of trade schools for young women and men each year.

I also want to acknowledge the resources and books that influenced and helped in the compilation of *Letters for Healing*. Some of these resources were referenced directly on these pages, but all provided valuable insights.

With Pen in Hand: The Healing Power of Writing by Henriette Anne Klauser;

What is Narrative Therapy? by Alice Morgan;

Personal Notes: How to Write From the Heart for Any Occasion by Sandra E. Lamb;

The Art of the Handwritten Note by Margaret Shepherd;

My Cross to Bear by Gregg Allman;

"The King is Dead; Long Live The King: Narrative Therapy and Practicing What We Preach" by R.E. Doan;

Narrative Means to Therapeutic Ends by Michael White and David Epston;

Maps of Narrative Practice by Michael White;

"Community Song Writing and Narrative Practice" (UK publication *Clinical Psychology*) by David Denborough;

"Guidelines for Writing Therapy" by Dr. Jim Byrne;

Collected Papers, James W. Pennebaker;

The Complete Papers and Writings of Abraham Lincoln: Constitutional Edition by Abraham Lincoln;

Men's Journal, November 2012, Greg Louganis interview by Sean Woods;

A Woman of Independent Means by Elizabeth Forsythe Hailey;

The Complete Poems of John Donne by John Donne;

The Complete Poems of Emily Dickinson by Emily Dickinson;

Anecdotes of the Late Samuel Johnson by Hester Lynch Piozzi (Henry Morley, editor);

The Year of Magical Thinking by Joan Didion;

Blue Nights by Joan Didion;

Healing the Pain of Pet Loss: Letters in Memoriam by Kymberly Smith;

"Imaginal Flooding in the Treatment of Post-Traumatic Stress Disorder" by T.M. Keane and D.G. Kaloupek (*Journal of Consulting and Clinical Psychology*, February 1982)

If you wish to submit a letter for consideration of placement in a future edition of the Letters for Healing series of books, please send the letter and your contact information to: The Letters Project Book, von_music@ hotmail.com. While we cannot guarantee every letter will be included we do promise to read every one.

FUTURE EDITIONS BEING CONSIDERED:

~ *Letters for Healing: Letters from Critically Ill Children about Themselves*

~ *Letters for Healing: Letters to Lost Pets*

~ *Letters for Healing: Letters to Those Lost in Service*

BY ELENA MIKHALKOVA

In difficult times, you move forward in small steps.
Do what you have to do, but little by little.
Don't think about the future, or what may happen tomorrow.
Wash the dishes.
Remove the dust.
Write a letter.
Make a soup.
You see?
You are advancing step by step.
Take a step and stop.
Rest a little.
Praise yourself.
Take another step.
Then another.

You won't notice, but your steps will grow more and more.
And the time will come when you can think
about the future without crying.

www.ingramcontent.com/pod-product-compliance
Lightning Source LLC
Chambersburg PA
CBHW031525120626
46545CB00005B/2000